KITCHEN PHYSICS

Dynamic Nigerian Recipes

DEJI BADIRU AND ISWAT BADIRU

KITCHEN PHYSICS:
DYNAMIC NIGERIAN RECIPES

iUniverse books may be ordered through booksellers or by contacting:

iUniverse
1663 Liberty Drive
Bloomington, IN 47403
www.iuniverse.com
1-800-Authors (1-800-288-4677)

ISBN: 978-1-5320-5421-1 (sc)
ISBN: 978-1-5320-5422-8 (e)

Library of Congress Control Number: 2018908354

Print information available on the last page.

iUniverse rev. date: 07/20/2018

Books in the ABICS Publications Book Series

(www.abicspublications.com)

Kitchen Physics: Dynamic Nigerian Recipes

The Story of Saint Finbarr's College: Contributions to Education and Sports Development in Nigeria

Physics of Soccer II: Science and Strategies for a Better Game

Kitchen Dynamics: The rice way

Consumer Economics: The value of dollars and sense for money management

Youth Soccer Training Slides: A Math and Science Approach

My Little Blue Book of Project Management

8 by 3 Paradigm for Time Management

Badiru's Equation of Student Success: Intelligence, Common Sense, and Self-discipline

Isi Cookbook: Collection of Easy Nigerian Recipes

Blessings of a Father: Education contributions of Father Slattery at Saint Finbarr's College

Physics in the Nigerian Kitchen: The Science, the Art, and the Recipes

The Physics of Soccer: Using Math and Science to Improve Your Game

Getting things done through project management

Dedication

In remembrance of Anthony Bourdain, who taught us the global human side of the kitchen.

Acknowledgments

We gratefully acknowledge the support, encouragement, and taste-testing services of Abi, John, Ade, Deanna, and Tunji.

INTRODUCTION

All About Food, Kitchen, and People

This is a recipe book with a unique twist. Unlike most conventional recipe books, "Kitchen Physics: Dynamic Nigerian Recipes" takes readers through an intellectual path of cooking popular Nigerian foods.

Food and recipes bring people together. Immigrants residing anywhere in the World connect with their original homelands through their continuing connection with their respective ethnic foods. No matter how long an immigrant has lived outside his or her home country, the excitement of relevant ethnic foods still persists. Even second, third, and fourth generation immigrants still connect with their parents' original home countries through the appropriate ethnic foods. This fact is very much applicable to Nigerian immigrants anywhere in the world. The purpose of this book is to provide an avenue of connectivity to the ethnic origins of readers. He or she who is connected to the food is connected to the ethnic affiliation of the food. Not forgetting home means connecting with foods from home. Food and fellowship go hand-in-hand in the African culture. There are facts and fallacies of food all around the world, but it is often fellowship that gels everything together. In that context, our kitchen prayer goes as follows:

"Give us life and love, fellowship and faith, and free pursuit of flavor."

Cultural Linkages in Food Evolution and Adaptation

Food and recipes bring people together. Immigrants residing anywhere in the World connect with their original homelands through their continuing connection with their respective ethnic foods. No matter how long an immigrant has lived outside his or her home country, the excitement of relevant ethnic foods still persists. Even second, third, and fourth generation immigrants still connect with their parents' original home countries through the appropriate ethnic foods. This fact is very much applicable to Nigerian immigrants anywhere in the world through cultural linkages in food evolution and adaptation. Kitchen physics provides an avenue of connectivity to the ethnic origins of readers. He or she who is connected to the food is connected to the ethnic affiliation of the food. Not forgetting home means connecting with foods from home. There is a lot of fun, facts, and fallacies in food fellowships across ethnic groups.

Tasting is Believing

This book allows you to feel and appreciate, and, hopefully, eventually see, feel, taste, and appreciate Nigerian recipes for yourself. Food appreciation boils down to seeing and tasting for yourself, like the marketing folks would say, "Seeing is believing; a trial will convince you."

Senses for Food Appreciation: Humans are endowed with complex and sophisticated biological sensors to provide a constant stream of environmental information, including position, orientation, and taste among many others. Food can be appreciated and enjoyed via any of the five senses of the human physiological makeup.

Touching: Experience the textual excellence of food.

Hearing: Hear the sizzle of cooking food and sensually get your palates ready.

Smelling: Feel the inviting aroma of food and imagine what is about to transpire.

Seeing: The sight of the visual presentation of food can make the food appetizing.

Tasting: It is through tasting that the gratification of food is manifested.

Through the sense of taste, humans have four primary discernments of food, namely bitter, sweet, sour, and salty. Our likes and dislikes are shaped by our inherent reactions to our savory perception of food.

For example, the love of chocolate is one avenue through which many people exercise all the senses of appreciation. Consider the comedic quotes below:

"A new British survey has revealed that 9 out of 10 people like chocolate. The tenth lies." - Robert Paul

"After about 20 years of marriage, I'm finally starting to scratch the surface of what women want. And I think the answer lies somewhere between conversation and chocolate." - Mel Gibson

It is fortuitous that we do have the discerning tastes because many of the things we savor are good for our health. Unfortunately, some are counter-productive to health. Tasty fat is one such adverse example. Salt, for another example, adds palate satisfaction to food while also meeting a basic requirement of adding an essential nutrient to our diet. Without the mineral provided by salt, humans cannot survive. Studies have shown that extreme low-sodium diets pose risks of possibly suffering from seizures and coma. Other studies have theorized that the love of the taste of chocolates has the side benefit of increasing metabolism, thus playing a role in weight loss. A 2012 study found that people who ate chocolates tend to weigh less. It is suspected that nutrients in chocolate may play a role in metabolism.

The late celebrity chef Anthony Bourdain traveled the world for the connectivity of food, culture, people, and fellowship. Bourdain highlighted the human moments behind each culinary scenario. That is really physics in the kitchen environment. At this point, we are reminded of Hoffman quote below:

"Good science only adds to the enjoyment of the culinary arts."

- Roald Hoffman, 1981 Nobel Laureate in Chemistry

Finger-licking Food

"When food is good, you don't need an intermediary for the full enjoyment. Get your fingers into the act directly." – Deji Badiru, June 2019

In many cultures around the world, before the advent of invented contraptions for eating, fingers were the natural and direct utensils. Many cultures still imbibe their foods with fingers. Even in advanced cultures, can you imagine eating hamburgers with mechanized utensils?

The spread of food from a Nigerian kitchen

Why Kitchen Physics?

The title of this book, "Kitchen Physics: Dynamic Nigerian Recipes," conveys both literary and figurative meanings. There is always the science of physics present in the kitchen and there is always dynamism in any kitchen that is worth its mettle. The kitchen is a very dynamic place in every home. It is the centroid of our existence. In mathematical terms, a centroid is the intersection point of a multi-faceted object. That, indeed, is what the kitchen represents in any home, whether bygone or modern. The kitchen is a special place in all cultures around the world. The best family traditions often start in the kitchen, as alluded to by the Reagan quote below:

> "All great change in America begins at the dinner table." – Ronald Reagan

More and more, the kitchen, with the emergence of "kitchen islands," is replacing the dining table. Families nowadays often congregate around the kitchen island for informal breakfast, brunch, lunch, and dinner. Sometimes, the island even doubles as a homework table for kids, particularly when left home alone.

Food, the product of the kitchen, is the pathway to our well-being and the channel for a fulfilled soul. As such, it is full of physics and dynamics. In the Nigerian kitchen, cooking is often a manifestation of passion rather than a mere necessity. Food is a universal language of well-being. Food sustains life. No human exists who does not have a need to eat. No one can practice perpetual complete abstinence from food. Since complete abstinence from food is not possible, we might as well embrace it, celebrate it, and pay homage to all the stages of food transformation; growing it, cultivating it, harvesting it, cooking it, consuming it, digesting it, and using it to nourish our bodies. No matter which side of the above opening quote you profess to stand, the fact remains that you have a close relationship with food. Cooking is like a well-orchestrated symphony, where carefully appointed ingredients play together in perfect harmony. The symphony director (aka the chef) is the pride of the kitchen.

The modern kitchen has as much drama and sentiments as the communal kitchen common in rural parts of Nigeria. There is a lot of dynamics that occur in every kitchen environment. In a rural communal kitchen, housewives congregate and interact to discuss current affairs in the household and debate community politics and gossips. Each household in the communal compound has its own stove or cooking spot in the shared space. So, the interplay of people, personalities, physical environment, and cooking equipment create memorable kitchen dynamics. As Anthony Bourdain used to tell us, street food kiosks, originating from local (often rural) kitchens are the best sources of exceptional culinary experiences.

Even in a single-family modern kitchen, where there is no sharing of cooking space, the family structure and residential personalities still create unique kitchen dynamics. Modern kitchen gadgets have simplified and expedited the preparation of food. Regardless of whichever kitchen structure prevails in the Nigerian household, the best foods still emanate as the end product. The Nigerian love and passion for food is evident in each type of kitchen. However, the complexity of Nigerian recipes often creates an impediment to non-Nigerians becoming proficient with the recipes. Thus, a good recipe book is very essential.

The Nigerian kitchen is a beehive of activities full of energy and cacophony of laughter, particularly during party preparations. Many a time, the dynamism of a Nigerian kitchen borders on mayhem. In spite of its chaotic and jumbled appearance, the kitchen puts out the best of the best of food preparation. This typifies the following Yoruba saying:

"Inu ikoko dudu ni eko funfun ti unjade."

This translates roughly to say, "It is from a black pot that white corn meal emanates." No matter how rural a Nigerian kitchen might be, it still produces the best meals. This saying is also often used to commend the career successes of children who have risen out of poverty.

The term, Physics, in the title of this book, is not just about the science of physics. Rather, the word epitomizes the dynamics (processes, actions, and interfaces) that exist in a kitchen environment. As readers will soon find out, the Nigerian kitchen can be full of drama, excitement, and cacophony. In the Nigerian kitchen, commotion is what breeds gastronomic excellence, particularly for large party preparations.

The Nigerian kitchen is full of drama and excitement. One sample of a kitchen excitement is one incident that our older kids (Abi and Ade) witnessed when they were teenagers. According to Deji's recollection, a female family friend, Ms. D, known to our kids as "auntie" came to our home for a visit. Upon entering the kitchen, she started jumping up and down shouting to Iswat in a mixed English-and-Yoruba tone:

"Auntie, auntie, meatpie yen. Tie ba towo, oh my Goodness. O da gan ni."

This means "the meatpie turned out great. If you taste it, it will feel like heaven. It is very good."

Abi and Ade ran out of their rooms to come and check what the commotion was all about. They have never forgotten the excitement of that moment . . . all for the sake of a good meat pie.

For the Love of Food

So pervasive is the topic of food preparation that it has become a favorite topic to write about. The prevalence of recipe books on the market attests to this fact. Along with writing children's books, writing recipe books has become a favorite pastime of celebrities both old and young. Maya Angelou, in 2010, at the age of 82, wrote the book, "Great food, all day long: Cook splendidly, eat smart." Mr. Al Roker, popularly known as America's favorite weatherman, also has written a few cookbooks. This book follows the tradition of documenting and commending food in all its forms. This book celebrates Nigerian cooking at its best. Even nature endorses human's love of food. By far, the hardest part of the human body is the outer layer of teeth, thus enabling humans to tackle even the toughest food challenges.

Food as a Centerpiece of Fellowship

Food is the centerpiece of fellowship in the African tradition. Nigerians take this rallying point to the next level in the way they host and entertain friends, family, neighbors, and extended acquaintances. Cooking and serving food is an essential part of how Nigerians promulgate fellowship.

From the Western, Eastern, Northern, and Southern nooks and corners of Nigeria, food is embraced and even worshiped in some local practices. Just as sports are often used as common basis to unify disparate parts of a developing nation, the common interest in food can also be used as a common basis to overcome the nagging political differences that are rampant in developing nations. Trade and commerce related to food are important elements of how communities and nations interact. From sharing food, exchanging recipes, and "*festivalizing*" food to creating community unions, food facilitates participatory alliances among people of all creed and color throughout the world. Mass feeding of everyone within reach is a trademark of Nigerian chefs (actually, all African chefs), which is mere demonstration of the passion of cooking for many. This book is the culmination of years of passion and dedication to the science and art of cooking by the husband-and-wife team of authors.

Market Scenes in Nigeria

Market scenes in Nigeria are exciting with a lot of fresh foods to offer. Fresh fish is common in the Nigerian diet. This implies frequent (or even daily) visits to the market. Not only do visitors to the market enjoy the drama surrounding market-price haggling for fresh fish, they also take delight in the spontaneous celebratory dancing and singing that occur in many a market in Nigeria. Fish, whether cooked fresh or smoked, is common in the Nigerian diet.

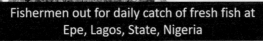

Fishermen out for daily catch of fresh fish at Epe, Lagos, State, Nigeria

Appreciation of Physics in the Kitchen

As farmers, even without the benefit of written theory, can tell us, a lot of physics happens in how water moves through a plant's roots, stems, and leaves to generate the unique characteristics that make them edible and delectable. The Nigerian diet, very much like the Asian diet, consists of many plant products (i.e., roots, stems, and leaves). So, plant physics essentially goes on behind the scene of the Nigerian food. Authors, Karl J. Niklas and Hanns-Christof Spatz commemorated the importance of plant physics with their 2012 book, **Plant Physics** (University of Chicago Press, Chicago, IL). Of a similar orientation is the 2007 book by Ludger O. Figura and Arthur A. Teixeira entitled **Food Physics: Physical Properties – Measurement and Applications** (Springer-Verlag, Berlin, Germany). Thus, the topic of physics, whether from the classical theory of physics or the more generic interpretation of dynamics, does play and important role in the kitchen. Therein lies the need to write about physics in the kitchen. Good chefs, even without a formal knowledge of physics, do understand how to leverage the physics, biology, and chemistry in each food source (e.g., water content, permeability, microbial properties, etc.) to achieve their culinary goals. Indigenous cooks in Nigeria and other developing countries, even without any formal education can cook up a marvel because they understand the inherent properties of their raw materials. That is kitchen physics! Although this book does not dwell on the classical principles of physics, it aims to inform, enlighten, and inspire the readers about what goes on behind-the-scene of food preparation in the Nigerian kitchen, or any other kitchen for that matter.

The premise of *"Kitchen Physics"* is the integration of the science, art, and passion of cooking. There is a lot of science behind the ingredients that go into cooking. While the book touches on physics as a science found in the kitchen, it is not about the subject of physics. The term physics, in this case, refers to the various activities that occur in the kitchen. Naturally, there is a lot of activities in the Nigerian kitchen. The literal interpretation of the title conveys the direct functional role of physics as a scientific tool in the kitchen. The figurative interpretation coveys the fact that the "physics" of something is often used to refer to how something is done; as in "how" to practice and execute kitchen chores. For this purpose, this book's title addresses fundamental "how-to" processes of carrying out a recipe in the kitchen touching on selection of ingredients, cooking time, food quality, quantity, storage, and so on.

Most ingredients undergo radical scientific transformation before reaching the final flavor at which we use them. In many cases, the intermediate stages of the transformation have their own uses in the cooking process as they can impact different levels of texture, visual appeal, flavor, and taste. For example, it is reported that fresh garlic, when minced can become spicy, however, when slightly sautéed or roasted, it becomes sweet.

The art of cooking relates to the skills of using the various ingredients in tactical combinations to arrive at the intended end goal of a recipe. Finally, it is the passion of cooking that brings out the best in every cook. Without the passion, the cooking effort is a mere abstraction of desire without a manifestation.

Physics in the Nigerian Kitchen is a marvelous fun book that intertwines humor with the serious business of preparing and eating food. It is written as an intellectual cookbook, not the convention common cookbook or recipe book. It is targeted at those who are very serious about cooking and curious enough to find out the science behind it. The book brings together the basic principles of physics and the art of cooking to create foods that satisfy the body and soul of any food lover. The title of the book not only conveys some food for thought, but also suggests science for imbibing, suitable for dining table conversations.

Food poisoning is rare in the Nigerian cuisine because rarely do we cook anything rare. Most foods are cooked well done. The Western practice of cooking meat rare or medium rare usually doesn't sit well with Nigerians. The practice of multiple hand washings is also common in the Nigerian kitchen because bare hands are used constantly throughout the cooking process. From hand-handling of meat to sprinkling of spices on the food, hands must be used again and again. In fact, in the final eating of the food, it is not uncommon to dispense of silverware in favor of digging in with bare fingers. That is actually the best way to enjoy many Nigerian delicacies. So, intuitively, hands are washed frequently.

To get ready for your cooking exposition, you need to review your kitchen and household scales and measurements presented below. What translates to what in kitchen measurements? We must admit that traditional Nigerians rarely cook by measurement. But in the global melting pots of recipe exchange, everyone needs a basic knowledge of ounce, pinch, and pint.

Once upon a time, there was a widespread tradition of sending a bride to fattening rooms, where they get fed and prevented from physical activity for the purpose of building up a plumper physique for the appreciation of the groom. That tradition has practically died out, overtaken by the modern health realities. Brides now desire a trim physique going into the courtship and wedding phases of their relationships. In a traditional fattening room, prospective brides are fed large amounts of food, massaged, and made to sleep for long periods of time in an effort to increase their weight and gain fuller proportions. Although this may still be practiced in some remote villages in certain parts of Nigeria, it is no longer looked upon favorably. In agreement with the modern reality of pursuing a healthy body, the authors provide the following piece of advice:

"Your weight is within your control if you take control early; before weight creep creeps in."

Along the same line, an oriental philosophy says:

"Always leave the table feeling like you could have eaten more."

It is essential to note that the best way to savor food is not to eat too much of it, at least, not all at once. If one eats to the point of being full, the sensory system becomes lethargic, shuts down, or slows down, thus, preventing the full enjoyment of the food. Note that serving size is more important than calorie and fat contents of the food.

After exercising all the senses of food appreciation, now comes the task of burning off the calories. It is treadmill time! Treadmills are fantastic for indoor calorie burn-off. Accumulated fat that refuses to dissipate of its own accord can be helped along with a good treadmill workout. While it is good to get out and workout in the open air occasionally, indoor treadmill workout offers convenience, privacy, and protection from the weather elements; not to talk of avoidance of neighborhood dogs seeking to take a swipe at joggers.

Food is often the culprit in many of our ailments, either in a wrong form, irrational quantity, or incompatible combination. The fact is that we don't need much food to sustain life. As much as the authors encourage eating well with diverse experimentations, it is recognized that food must be consumed in moderation. Laboratory studies as well as direct human observations tend to suggest that consistently consuming large quantities of food can adversely affect life span. Not only does a large quantity of food blatantly task the body's digestive system, it also means that whatever unfavorable contents lurk in the food end up bombarding the body mechanisms more aggressively. Over a long stretch of time, these adverse impacts manifest themselves in all sorts of diseases whose root causes are difficult to trace. External impacts can be seen through visual assessment of size (e.g., obesity) while internal impacts are often unnoticeable until it is too late. So, the basic lesson offered by this book is to experiment with food (cooking, tasting, consuming, etc.), but also give the body a fighting chance against the unwanted side effects noted above. Eating less not only has positive effect on weight, but also helps to wade off potential sources of pathogens by reducing the type and volume of what is ingested. The quotes below seem appropriate in this regard:

"Some live to eat, some eat to live."

   - Classical saying, source unknown

"A diet is when you watch what you eat and wish you could eat what you watch."

   - Hermione Gingold

"A fully gorged belly never produced a sprightly mind."

- Jeremy Taylor

"A good meal ought to begin with hunger."

- French Proverb

"A hungry stomach seldom scorns plain food."

- Horace

"Lead me not into temptation (of food), I can find the way myself." – Rita Mae Brown

Note: The "of food" insertion is due to the authors.

It is known that some people eat more when they eat with other people while some eat less when they eat alone. Of course, we would always have those who eat against the grains in these standardized expectations. When you eat less alone, it is probably because you don't have to impress alone with your appetite. When you eat more alone, it is probably because you lack self-discipline and you would gorge yourself if no one is watching. In the case of those who eat more in a group, it is often because of what these authors call **competitive cyclic psychology** of filling up the plate. This is how it happens, particularly in smorgasbord restaurants that serve a large variety of buffet items. One person gawks at the other person's plate and thinks 'gee, he got more than I got,' and the reacts by pilling more food onto his own plate. This sends a subliminal message. Of course, the second person subconsciously notices that he is being beaten in the unspoken and unannounced eating competition and decides to retaliate by piling on more food. This *strike-back* mentality can go on back and forth until each person has overdone it, thereby fueling the wheels of obesity subconsciously. Sometimes it is someone desiring to eat more who gets the competition started. This instigator might say 'is that all you got? Get more, we have plenty of food you know' and urges others to fill their plates more. He or she then uses any gullible responders as an excuse to then pile up more food onto his or her own plate.

Children are particularly prone to the type of competitive eating psychology described here. There is a **scarcity mentality** that lurks somewhere in all of us, and it does not apply only to food. It tells us to grab all we can; otherwise, someone else will grab it all. This is very rampant and socially damaging in developing countries where basic resources are in limited supply to begin with. So, how do we combat this psychology of stuffing the plate? The author's simple advice is to **mind your own plate**. Don't look around the table for benchmarks. And don't be swayed by the clash of gastronomic aroma at the buffet table.

Heart disease is one of the most-feared ailments. It is often a side effect of a sedentary lifestyle. We can control the effects of our lifestyle by eating the right foods. It is quite often difficult to change our lifestyles drastically over a short period of time; but we can incrementally modify our eating habits to ensure we are protecting our hearts. With some mindful eating, we can reduce our risk of heart disease. The super foods listed below, which contain beneficial fats, fiber, antioxidants, essential vitamins, and minerals, protect our hearts by lowering blood pressure, increasing good cholesterol and helping to prevent the build-up of plaque in arteries. Please, keep these super foods in mind the next time you're planning a meal. Yes, they go well with **Nigerian dishes** too!

There is often a conflict between what our taste buds want and what our bodies need. To emphasize this, co-author Deji created the original quote below to convey his own perception of this conundrum,

> *"Nature has a twisted sense of humor. Whatever is good for our taste buds is often not good for our body."* - Deji Badiru, Dec 30, 2007

It is true that foods that taste the best are not often the best foods for us health-wise. As good taste increases, so does the health risk. Below are some tips and facts on food, health, and body.

1. Black beans: Black beans are packed with folate, antioxidants, and magnesium, which are good for lowering blood pressure, blood sugar and cholesterol. This in turn keeps your heart in the safe zone. But if you are planning to use canned beans, be sure to drain the liquid and wash them before use to reduce the sodium content.

2. Salmon and tuna: These two fish are rich in anti-oxidants and omega-3, two essential requirements for heart health.

3. Walnuts: A handful of them a day helps lower your cholesterol and reduce inflammation in the arteries. Use them as replacement for in-between-meals snacks, instead of chips, etc.

4. Oranges: They contain cholesterol-fighting pectin. The fruit is also rich in potassium that helps control blood pressure. Antioxidant hesperidin also helps lower blood pressure.

5. Carrots: Though sweet, they are good to control diabetes, which increases the risk of heart attack. They also help fight bad cholesterol.

6. Sweet potatoes: They are rich in vitamin A, fiber, and lycopene, making them a healthy substitute for white potatoes.

7. Oats: Oats in all forms help your heart by lowering bad cholesterol. **Oats for Life**: Oat meal can, indeed, be a full meal. Oats are known to be a good source of dietary fiber.

8. Flaxseeds: These contain fiber, photo chemicals, called lignans, and ALA. These three ingredients in these small seeds make the seeds a powerhouse of health. They can be very helpful if used in powdered form every day in cereals or salads.

9. Chili powder: It is hard to believe, but this Nigerian tasty spice actually protects the heart from disease and the body from diabetes with its ability to spike up the natural insulin levels in the body.

10. Coffee: It can reduce Type 2 diabetes, but those with high blood pressure should be cautious as it can have a counter effect on blood pressure levels.

Diversification is of utmost importance for good life and soul health. Even if you love processed fast foods, just make sure it is not your only staple food source.

When we say foods for life, we literally mean preserving life. Immunity boosters offer one avenue to life preservation. It is important to choose foods that boost the immune system. Fresh fruits and vegetables are a good source of immunity boosters. When consumed year-round as a part of a well-balanced diet, fruits and vegetables provide good protection against common viruses. Some typical examples are presented below:

Vitamin C: This is an anti-oxidant that protects cells by neutralizing the damaging effects of free radicals. It also facilitates resistance to inflection. Sources of Vitamin C include citrus, berries, red and green bell peppers, tomatoes, red cabbage, kale, parsley, collards, broccoli, and spinach.

Vitamin E: This is an antioxidant that protects against cell membrane damage. It has a protective effect against viral infections, such as the common cold. Sources of Vitamin E include wheat germ oil, green leafy vegetables, almonds, hazelnuts, whole grains, and avocados.

Zinc: This stimulates the immune system and inhibits viruses by increasing the number of infection-fighting T-cells. Good sources of zinc include beans, pumpkin seeds, split peas, Brazil nuts, whole grains, almonds, walnuts, garlic, and carrots.

Oh, garlic has other benefits also as suggested by an old New York proverb:

"A nickel will get you on the subway, but garlic will get you a seat."

 - Old New York Proverb

Todd Easton advises that the best way to maintain a healthy diet habit is to know when to do or eat what. His book entitled "The When Diet: Mathematically Optimizing Eating and Exercise for Weight Loss" (Ithaca Press, New York, NY, 2009) presents mathematical reasoning to optimize eating and exercise for weight loss. He opines that from a mathematically-rigorous decision theory point of view, it makes no sense to be on a diet if the diet causes more harm than the benefit derived from the weight-loss goal of dieting.

It is highly encouraged to add fiber to our diet. High-fiber diet is helpful for prevention and treatment of certain intestinal diseases especially diverticulosis, hemorrhoids, constipation, and irritable bowel syndrome. High-fiber diets have the following benefits:

- Decrease in time it takes for food waste to move through the body's digestive system

- Decrease in bowel pressure

- Production of better bowel movement

The following suggestions for high-fiber diets are culled from several sources:

1. Whenever possible, use whole grain breads instead of refined white breads.

2. Use whole wheat pasta (macaroni and noodles) and brown rice instead of white rice and whole grain cornmeal for cornbread.

3. Eat dried beans, peas, and corn more often.

4. Add two tablespoons unprocessed wheat bran to daily consumption.

5. Eat edible peeling of vegetables and fruits.

6. Select raw and fresh fruits and vegetables more often. Note that cooking reduces some of the fiber in foods.

7. Drink six to eight glasses of liquid (preferably water) each day.

8. Gradually introduce fibrous foods into diet and increase amounts as can be tolerated.

9. Eat selected nuts and seeds to add balance to diet.

10. Use high fiber cereal following the tabulated guide below:

Vegetables are high in **fiber** and Nigerians eat a lot of it. Nigerian-made flour is also fiber packed and common in the Nigerian diet. Below is a sampling of high-fiber foods common in the Nigerian diet.

- Dried beans

- Black beans

  Dried fruit

  Raspberries, blackberries and strawberries

  Oats

- Bread

  Baked potato with the skin

- Mashed and boiled potatoes

  Raisins and prunes: Not as high on the list as other dried fruits (see #5) however valuable.

  Greens: Spinach, beet greens, kale, collards, turnip greens, etc.

  Nuts

  Cherries

  Bananas

  Carrots

  Coconut

All in all, kitchen physics brings together the multitude of factors and emotions needed to arrive at extraordinary food products. Readers are encouraged to maintain an open mind, broad thinking, and welcoming eyes to appreciate the joys offered by Nigerian recipes.

This chapter describes some of the most popular ingredients and accompaniments seen in Nigerian recipes. Most of the ingredients here can be obtained in supermarkets although some items may only be found in African food shops.

- **Afang / Ukazi leaves (gnetum African)**

  Dark green Shiny foliage of the creeping afang plant cultivated mostly in Calabar and Igbo land are used a great deal in the cooking of these regions. It can be bought ready shredded from African food stores.

- **Atama leaves/Beletientien**

  This is an annual Herb cultivated in the delta areas. It smells and taste like tarragon; usually used fresh or dried in Banga soup. Use dried leaves sparingly as flavor is more intense. Readily available from African food stores.

- **Avocado (persea Americana)**

  Tropical fruit with thick warty skin usually greenish or purplish in color. The edible flesh inside surrounds a large oval shape seed. It is light yellow and soft when ripe. Avocados can be eaten on its own or cut in half and filled with cooked seafood (Avocado and prawn cocktail).

- **Beans or Cowpeas**

Black-eye beans or Brown beans have become indispensable in Nigeria cuisine because of it versatility in use. It requires overnight soaking before use for dishes like Akara Moin-mom and Gbegiri soup.

- **Banana**

This is one of the most important food crops in Nigeria. Widely eaten on it's own or in fruit salads they make a good substitute for plantains. The leaves are usually used for wrapping foods such as Anyan-Ekpang or Ebiripo for steaming. Baking foil or greased parchment paper make adequate substitute but do not add the delicate flavour that banana leaves give.

- **Bitterleaf**

A leafy green vegetable that is widely used in soups like Egusi for its bitter but sweet flavor. The fresh leaves is prepared like spinach and washed with salt; rubbing and squeezing to remove some of the bitterness before use. Can be bought fresh or ready washed and air-dried.

- **Chilli Peppers**

Chilli peppers are the fruit of Capsicum Frutescens plant with red orange or yellow pods which are very hot rich in Vitamin A & C and widely used in Nigerian cooking. While the flavor in the chilli lies in the flesh and skins much of the heat potency rests in the seeds and veins which can be removed. Green chillies are a lot hotter than the red ones. The active chemical con stituent is capiasin renowned for stimulating digestive process and helping to relieve heat fatigue in hot climates by inducing perspiration.

- **Breadfruit**

These are large green fruits which hang like lanterns from tress. Only edible when cooked and taste like boiled potatoes. It could also be fried as crisp.

- **Cassava (Manihot esculenta)**

Cassava is a tropical vegetable with a long tu berous root and dull green palmate leaves. Mature tubers have brown mottled skin with a white fibrous flesh. It can be cooked and eaten with coconut (Eberebe); but mostly used for making Gad (Cassava grains) and Fufu. Used as accompaniment to soups and stews. It can be bought ready-made as gaff or cassava flour (Fufu).

- **Cocoyam**

  Cocoyams are similar to large potatoes usually with a fibrous skin. In Nigeria the plant is grown for both its tubers and leaves. The young and tender leaves are used in preparing Ekpang Nkukwo (cocoa-yam pottage). Spinach leaves make adequate substitute. These tubers can also be boiled roasted or fried.

- **Corn/Maize**

  Sweet corn or maize as it is commonly known is grown throughout Nigeria as a food source. The plant grows to a height of about seven feet. When fully mature, the swollen fruits are called cobs and it is these, which are picked and used for food. The cobs can be boiled, roasted, or cooked with beans as a main course. A number of by products are obtained from the grains including ogi (corn-starch) and corn oil, which is low in saturates and cholesterol.

- **Crayfish**

  Smoked dried prawns or shrips used for flavoring soups and savory dishes. Usually whole or ground.

- **Egusi (cirullus colocynthis) melon seeds**

  Seed of the African melon fruit used in preparing Egusi soup. Should be grinded before use. Can be oily but adds a nutty flavor to the soup.

- **Ewedu (corchorus olitorius)**

  Shiny green leave vegetable rich in Vitamins A C & D. Use in making sauces to accompany stews and enjoyed for its mucilaginous or viscous properties. Sold fresh or dried.

- **Elubo**

  Dried powdered yam flour for making amala (cooked yam flour pudding).

- **Fufu**

  Fermented cassava dough usually served cooked to accompany soups

- **Garden eggs (solanum melongena)**

  Also knows as African eggplant a member of the aubergine family. A round shiny green and yel low fruit with a slightly bitter taste. Garden eggs are eaten raw as a fruit or diced and added to stews.

- **Groundnut (Arachis hypogaea)**

Like a set of twins groundnut mature together in light coloured shells which are flaky and easy to break. Grown profusely in Northern Nigeria the seeds are harvested for their oil and protein. They can be eaten raw boiled roasted and pureed for making groundnut soup. Groundnut oil is used for cooking.

- **Iru (locust bean) parkia biglobosa**

Fermented locust or black beans. They have a slightly salty taste and a pungent smell. They are used as seasoning in soups. Usually sold fresh or dried packed.

- **Kaun (Rock salt) potash**

Usually added to food especially pulses during cooking for faster tenderisation and to increase the viscosity In Okro and Ewedu sauce. Also used for emulsifying oil and water in some traditional soups.

- **Mango (mangifera indica)**

This kidney shaped fruit is pinkish or yellowish in colour. When fully ripe it is lusciously sweet and succulent with the golden flesh. Mango is common in fruit platters and salad.

- **Millet (pennisetum)**

Tiny yellow grains obtained from plant that looks like bull rushes with a maize like stalk. Grows widely in Northern Nigeria and used mostly for porridge and gruel.

- **Okro (lady fingers)**

These vegetables are curved seed pod up to 9 inches Long they are usually eaten cooked in soup and salads.

- **Apon (ogbono Seed)**

This seeds are obtained from the nuts of the African mango bush and air dried in the sun. It has a subtle aromatic flavor and it's very mucilaginous when cooked. Can be bought whole or powdered.

- **Pawpaw (Carica papaya)**

This is a fruit of woody herbaceous plant that looks like a tree. It is eaten ripe (yellow or orange in color) in fruit salads or stuffed for starters or main course.

- **Plantain**

  A large member of the banana family plantain is less sweet than banana and is more versatile in use. It is often boiled toasted or fried and served with meat stews because the tissue has a starchy taste than sweet banana. It is best cooked with plenty of spices onions tomatoes and peppers (plantain pottage).

- **Ugwu (Pumpkin leaves) telfairi occidentallis**

  These trailing green leaves of the pumpkin plant rich in minerals and vitamins. Use in various soup preparations It is the chief ingredient in cooking Edikang Ikong soup. Fresh spinach can be used as substitute in any recipe if not available. Pumpkin seeds can also be eaten.

- **Utazi leaves (crongromena ratifolia)**

  This is a bitter tasting pale green leaf usually used for flavouring pepper soup. Very sparingly used. It can also be used as a substitute for bitter leaves.

- **Uzouza leaves or Ikong Etinkinrin**

  This sweet smelling aromatic and spicy pale green leaf vegetable is also used for flavoring soups especially (Ibaba soup).

- **Yam (Dioscorea sp)**

  The plant grows as a vine to height of six to eight feet. The edible tubers comes in various shapes and sizes; usually dark brown in color and hairy to the touch. The flesh is white or yellow and when cooked it has a pleasant flavor when cooked rather like potato. It is harvested in dry season with a gig feast known as Yam Festival in Igbo land. Yam still forms the staple diet of a large number of people in Nigeria. It is cooked in different ways including boiled roasted and fried. When pounded it is served as accompaniment to soups and stews.

- **Sorghum**

  Also known as guinea corn sorghum is cultivated mainly in Northern Nigeria. Used for porridge or pap (gruel).

- **Snail**

  These are large forest creatures covered with a hard shell. Taste rubbery when overcooked it is rather an acquired taste.

- **Oils**

  From a health stand point fats and oils are either saturated or unsaturated. Saturated oils such as butter coconut and palm oil are known to increase the amount of cholesterol carried in the blood but since regional cuisine is characterized by the type of oil used lesser quantities or half the amount in a given recipe could always be used.

- **Groundnut oil**

  This is used for frying and also added to stews and other savory dishes. It has a pleasant and unobtrusive taste; favorable in making mayonnaise and could be heated to a high temperature without burning.

- **Corn oil**

  This oil pressed from the germ of germ of maize (corn) is high in poly unsaturated and low in cholesterol. It is used the same way as groundnut oil. It can also be heated to a high temperature without burning.

- **Palm oil**

  This rather tasty and nutty thick and waxy rustic red colored oil is extracted from the flesh of the oil-palm nut fruits. It is widely used in Nigerian cooking especially in the traditional soups and stews for color and taste but usually in small quantity as it is high in saturates.

- **Water leaf (talilum triangulare)**

  This is the most widely used of all green leaf vegetables. It is rich in iron calcium and vitamin A and C and it is best eaten lightly cooked in soups and stews. spinach can be used in recipes calling for waterleaf.

- **Kuka leaves**

  Leaves of the baobab tree usually sold dried in powder form and used for Kuka soup.

- **IGBO (garden egg leaves) solanum manocarpum**

  The young leaves of the garden eggplant. African Aubergines can be eaten raw in salads or cooked in stews.

- **Soko (celosia argentea)**

  This green leaf vegetable is much preferred in the making of Efo-riro. It tastes like spinach.

- **Tete (celosia viddis)**

  This green is a close relative to Soko and is used interchangeable or in combination with it. It is widely grown in Western Nigeria.

- **Nutritious Okra**

  Okra is a shrub that grows to about two meters with yellow flower and succulent seed pod emanating from the flower. Both the leaves and the seed pod are major ingredients in several local dishes across West African countries. The seed pod is used to thicken soup, stews and sauces. The roasted seed can serve as coffee substitute. Because of its high fiber content, the stem is used in making paper. As a green vegetable, it is a good source of Iron, Vitamin C, Calcium and dietary fiber.

Fibrous Garri

Garri is the main staple food in many parts of Nigeria. It is more popular, more accessible, and more affordable than rice in the local diet. Its high dietary fiber content makes it a healthier alternative to rice. Garri (aka Gari) is composed of white or golden yellow crispy granules made from freshly harvested, milled, fermented, and fried cassava tubers or roots. It is a fine-to-coarse granular flour of with various levels of texture. The cassava roots go through the following processing steps after harvesting:

- Cleaning
- Grating
- De-moisturing (by squeezing out liquid)
- Fermenting
- Dehydrating (by dry-frying with or without palm oil)

Garri is eaten in a variety of ways, including soaking in water (super-saturated) and eating it very much like oatmeal. It is a fast, inexpensive, and refreshing food, particularly on a hot day. The accompaniment for eating garri this way include sugar, dry-roasted peanuts, milk, moin-moin, smoked fish, fried meat, and so on. Garri is used in making Eba by pouring and mixing it in boiling water. The resulting thick paste is eaten with meat and/or fish stews. Garri can come as white or yellow garri. White garri is obtained when the processing is done without the addition of red palm oil. The addition of palm oil helps to reduce and neutralize the cyanide content in cassava. Most white garri are fried and made safe to eat by allowing it to ferment over a longer period of time than usual.

The authors advocate a more adventurous engagement of cooking, beyond conventional recipes and cooking practices. Readers are encouraged to try something new, substitute uncharted ingredients, and experiment with modern healthy choices.

The traditional African recipes that call for the use of palm oil can be revolutionized with olive oil, canola oil, corn oil, peanut oil, or coconut oil. Who knows, a new favorite taste may be discovered. A bit of this, a dash of that, and a sprinkle of spices can lead to new recipe discoveries. Men should, however, be cautious when conducting recipe experiments in the presence of their better halves ---- unless there a cop out or a defensible position. The following conversation between the co-authors attests to this suggestion:

Man:	"Hymm, this did not turn out as I wished."
Woman:	"Wishful thinking does not a recipe make. Now, you've ruined a perfectly good fish."
Man:	"Well, I learned something new from the experiment."
Woman:	"What would that happen to be???"
Man:	"Never to try that again."

In spite of the failed experiments, don't be shy. Go ahead and try something new. A wise man once said:

"Don't quit. Success is failure turned inside out."

So, try and try again. Culinary success may be lurking in the next pot of soup. The photo below shows examples of specialty soup ingredients. Experimentation is the key.

What would have happened if someone so long ago did not experiment to discover the effect of salt on food flavor or the impact of sugar on the taste of tea? How did we discover the kicks of various spices?

In dancing, we can show that the art form of dancing is akin to the special art form of cooking . . . with measured steps serving as ingredients for a visually pleasing rumba.

Similarly, writing, which is akin to cooking and dancing, uses carefully selected words to compose sentences, which are choreographed to form articulate paragraphs, which eventually form a prose. Painting follows the same form as a composition of carefully selected shades of color.

Co-author, Deji, whose avowed hobbies include "food science experiments," regularly conducts kitchen research. Some turn out great while most turn out to belong on the shelf of lessons learned. He sees every failed cooking experiment as a lesson of what not to try in the future. Research and experimentation are essential for creating new and exciting dishes. A family friend commented to the authors "I think of you when I am trying new recipes in my kitchen." This is a compliment the authors are proud of. Deji is often the bold experimenter while Iswat is the development expert, who puts finishing touches to the new culinary ideas. One of our innovative ideas shared with friends and family includes bite-size puff-puff fries.

Food is a unifying element in family relationships. It brings us together in times of trouble and in times of joy. We celebrate with food. We celebrate food. In a talk about her book, *Recipes for Life,* Dynasty actress Linda Evans says she incorporates memories in her memoir with two of her favorite things --- cooking and eating. It seems to us that she endorses the new movement of "eatertainment."

Eating is one act that is common to all humans --- all living things for that matter. Even after a period of extended fasting, what follows is extreme engagement in eating. The act of eating will never go out of vogue. This is why we should celebrate it and write about it.

Of the body, eating provides nourishments that are essential for life, healing, and thriving as a social being.

Of the soul, eating offers pleasure that excites the senses that makes a person what he or she is spiritually and socially. While the body represents the engagement of time and space, it is the soul that creates the aura that ties everything together. Essentially, the soul is the atmosphere, spiritual or otherwise, within which the body resides.

Of the mind, eating expands the mind both through the anticipatory comfort of the food as well as the gratification of going through the action of consumption. A dull mind can result from not being exposed to a wide variety of food. One of the most cherished and desired by of garri is Ijebu Garri, which is authentically made in the Ijebu region of Nigeria. What makes Ijebu-Garri so special is the fact that it is left to ferment for much longer, thus generating the characteristic sour taste. The more sour the garri, the more desirable it is. The effect of prolonged fermentation is twofold. One purpose is to further reduce the carbohydrate (starch) content while the probiotic benefits are enhanced. As bacterial population increases the longer the fermentation process. Probiotics denotes a substance which stimulates the growth of microorganisms, especially those with beneficial properties (such as those of the intestinal flora). Ijebu-Garri is also dehydrated to a greater extent which further reduces the risk of molds giving it a longer shelf life.

Body of Water

Water is represented by the chemical symbol, H_2O (Hydrogen Monoxide: two molecules of hydrogen and one molecule of oxygen). It is the all-important and much-cherished water in any kitchen. The importance of water fits the theme of this book: Kitchen Physics. Pure water is odorless, tasteless, and clear. Water is one of nature's most important resources. Our survival depends on drinking water. Water is one of the most essential elements to good health, absorption of food, and digestion. Water also helps to maintain proper muscle tone and helps to convey oxygen and nutrients to cells in the body. Water also rids the body of wastes. For those concerned about their waist lines, it is important to note that water contains no calories. Although water covers more than 70% of the Earth, only 1% of the Earth's water is available as potable water for drinking. So, it is essential to conserve water at every opportunity. Excessive and unnecessary uses of water in the kitchen and bathroom must be avoided.

<u>Key properties of water</u>

- Freezing point of water: 0° C (32° F)

- Boiling point of water: 100° C (212° F).

- Water reaches its maximum density at 4° C (39° F)

- Water expands upon freezing

Water combines with salts to form hydrates and reacts with metal oxides to form acids Occurrence: Water is the only substance that occurs at ordinary temperatures in all three states of matter: solid, liquid, and gas.

"Body of Water" figuratively and biologically refers to the water composition of the human body. The body contains between 55% and 78% depending of body size. Water is a common chemical substance that makes our body healthy. It is composed of hydrogen and oxygen and it is very essential for life. Drinking plenty of water throughout the day helps replenish the water level in the body. It is, thus, essential for body and soul. Lean muscle tissue contains about 99% water by weight. Blood contains almost 50% water, body fat contains 1/2% water and bone has 97% water. Skin also contains much water. On the average, the human body is about 60% water in adult males and 55% in adult females. The fact below may be of interest.

Salt in Boiling Water

Water and salt are two of the most important essentials in a kitchen. It is interesting to note how they interact to do what we expect of them in terms of our food preparation. The effect of salt on the boiling point of water is particularly of interest, but only for theoretical reasons. For practical kitchen applications, the effect is negligible. But for scientific curiosity, we will examine the effect. Adding salt to water increases the boiling temperature (i.e., boiling point), causing the water to come to a boil more slowly. That is, it requires a higher temperature to boil. This increase in the cooking temperature will cause foods boiled in salt water to cook faster. Pure liquids (e.g., water) will generally have lower boiling points than mixtures (e.g., water and salt). For this reason, adding sugar to water has the same increasing effect on the boiling point as adding salt. If pure water is heated up to a high temperature prior to the addition of the salt, it could cause the entire pot to start boiling spontaneously. This is a result of the grains of salt acting as nucleation sites. This has the effect of making nearly-boiling water actually boil more quickly when salt is added. The tiny amount of salt required to cause a nucleation effect would have no effect on the temperature of the boiling water. In this regard, you can think of the salt as a catalyst, facilitating the change of state of the water from liquid to boiling.

Adding salt to water to raise the boiling point for cooking is actually negligible in practice. The amount of salt we normally add to water for typical cooking would have negligible effect on the boiling temperature. To easily remember this relationship, we present the visual plot below, based on a simple lab experiment. For fun experimentation purposes, you can add a few grains of salt to pure water to kick off the boiling process with nucleation; but beyond that, it will not have any noticeable effect on cooking temperature or time.

Temperature and Flavor: Temperature affects flavor. As reported by the November 2012 issue of Reader's Digest, researchers in Belgium found that certain taste bud receptors are most sensitive to food molecules that are at or just above room temperature. So, hot coffee may seem less bitter (i.e., tastes better) because our bitter-detecting taste buds are not as sensitive when coffee is hot. It was also found that odors also influence flavor. Thus, even the most bitter hot coffee may taste delicious because of its pleasant aroma. Coffee at room temperature does not have the same aroma.

Growly Stomach: What makes a stomach growl? It is believed that the digestive chemicals in the stomach churn and make stomach muscles to contract as they get prepped for food. Subconscious mental anticipation can cause muscle reflexes whether you want it or not. Consider the uncontrollable pee-pee urgency that develops as you approach a point of relief (aka the toilet), which can lead to the famous pee-pee dance. To mitigate a growly stomach, eat smaller meals more frequently.

Tips for Cooking Meats

- Meats are best if purchased fresh and used the day of, or within a day of purchase

- Always check the "Best if used by" date on the meat packaging for the freshest meats. Meats begin to lose flavor and spoil if you don't use them within 2- 3 days of purchase.

- Look for fat marbling in fresh beef. The fat adds more flavor, juiciness and tenderness to meats. But too much fat is strongly discouraged.

- Meats labeled "Reduced for Quick Sale" should be purchased only if you plan to use the meat the day of purchase. If possible, never buy meats that are out of date. The flavor and safety could be at risk.

- Fresh meat should be stored unwrapped or wrapped loosely in waxed paper, plastic wrap, paper wrap or aluminum foil. This allows the air to partially dry the surface of the meat and retard bacteria growth.

- Cured and smoked meats, sausages and ready-to-serve meats can be stored in their original wrappings.

- Cooked meat should be refrigerated quickly. Do not allow cooked meats to rest at room temperature for extended amounts of time. Room temperature will hasten bacterial growth on cooked meats, as well as uncooked meats.

- Do not freeze canned meats.

- To defrost frozen meats, always allow time to thaw in the refrigerator. Bacteria begins to grow on meats thawing at room temperature, therefore the meat becomes unsafe.

- Frozen meats can be cooked directly from the freezer, but the cooking time should be extended by up to 1/3 the normal amount of time for thawed or fresh meats.

- Using the correct cooking method for meats will optimize flavor and tenderness. This is good physics!

- When slicing meat, always cut **against** the grain of the meat. This will make the slices that are served more tender and easier to chew. Cutting meat with the grain will make meat stringy and it will seem tougher.

- When cutting raw meat, do not re-use the same cutting utensils during the cooking or eating process. Always use separate, clean utensils for raw and cooked meat. When cutting raw meat on a cutting board, do not cut cooked meat on the same board unless it has been washed thoroughly in Hot, Soapy water! Bacteria can be easily transferred to the cooked meat you are about to serve.

- When raw meat is placed on a plate or platter and taken to your outdoor grill, do not place the grilled meat back on the same plate or platter. Either wash the platter in hot, soapy water first, or use a clean platter.

- When marinating meat, discard the leftover marinade after you remove the meat.

- Never serve the raw meat marinade on your cooked meat.

- Some raw meat marinades can be cooked and served after the raw meat has been removed from it. Once a marinade has been cooked, it is safe. The extreme heat during the cooking process will kill any and all possible traces of bacteria that may have grown during the marinating process.

General Kitchen Tips

- Fresh eggs have rough, chalky shells. If the shell is smooth and shiny, it's old.

- The whites of poached or boiled eggs won't run if you add a teaspoon of vinegar to the water when boiling.

- To determine if that loose egg in the refrigerator is hard-boiled, spin it. If it spins on the countertop, it's hard-boiled. If it wobbles around, it's raw.

- Eggs at room temperature beat up fluffier.

- For easy removal of shells from hard-boiled eggs, immerse them in ice-cold water for about 5- 10 minutes before shelling.

- If baked meringue (whipped egg whites) is runny, add 1 teaspoon of cornstarch to the sugar before beating it into the egg whites.

- Before baking your meringue, sprinkle 2 teaspoons of granulated sugar over the top.

- This make for easier slicing and less tearing of the browned peaks.

- Use medium to large eggs in your recipes. Extra-large eggs may cause a cake to fall somewhat after it has cooled.

Here is fun "Why" question composed by the first author:

"Why do some hens have eggs?"

"Because they go brown nosing in the dirt."

- When frying bacon, separate the slices in the package by rolling it up before opening it.

- Bacon won't curl as bad when you fry it if you dip it into cold water first. Don't put it into hot grease.

- Lemons give more juice if they are at room-temperature before slicing.

- Store popcorn in your freezer. This will make almost every kernel to pop.

- If the center of your hamburger is not done, when patting out burger patties, make a hole in the center with your finger. This prevents the "puffy" raw center. If you freeze hamburger patties for later use, make sure to make a hole before freezing.

- Thaw fish in milk for a "fresh fish" taste.

- If creamed-corn is stuck on the bottom of your pan, add water and boil for easy removal. This works well with casserole dishes in the oven, as well.

- Remove lime deposits from pots, tea kettles and coffee pots by cleaning with equal parts vinegar and water.

- Clean silver with a damp cloth and baking soda.

- Old toothbrushes are wonderful kitchen and bathroom helpers in those small. hard-to- reach places. Please clean old brushes thoroughly before using in the kitchen.

- If drain is clogged with grease, pour down a cup each of salt and baking soda followed by a pot of boiling water.

- Keep your septic tank healthy by pouring buttermilk in your drain once a month.

- If your brown sugar has hardened, place a slice of apple in the container.

- Tear less when cutting your onions by working from the top down to the root end.

- Remove the core from a head of lettuce by hitting the core end sharply on the counter.

- Lettuce and celery keep longer in a paper lunch bag instead of the plastic wrap.

- To absorb grease in a pot of homemade soup, drop in a lettuce leaf. It will attract the grease. Dispose of leaf before consuming the soup.

- Drop a few ice cubes in the soup, they will also collect excess grease. Remove them quickly before they melt.

- If you have over-salted soup or veggies, add a few cut-up raw potatoes. They absorb excess salt. Discard the potatoes.

- Adding a teaspoon of sugar and a teaspoon of cider vinegar to over-salted vegetables or soup will also help dilute the salt content.

- If your gravy turns out lumpy, brown the flour well before adding your liquid. Whisk well.

- If you have greasy gravy, add 1/4 teaspoon of baking soda.

- Fresh whipped cream whips up better if you chill the cream, bowl and beaters.

- If you have runny whipped cream, add an egg white and chill. Re-beat and it will fluff up again.

- Add a few drops of lemon juice to whipping cream to make it whip up better.

- Add a few drops of lemon juice to simmering rice to keep the grains separated.

- When sautéing or panfrying, always heat the pan first before adding the oil or butter.

- If your pasta or rice is boiling over, adding 2 teaspoons of butter or oil will prevent this. You can also grease the top couple of inches of your pot before you add water to boil.

- When spooning out shortening, run the spoon under hot water and it will release easily.

- When broiling, add water to the pan section to prevent the grease from burning to the bottom of the pan and for easier clean-up.

- If tomatoes are not ripe enough, put them in a brown lunch bag and close. Keep at room temperature for a few days to hasten ripening.

- Remove skin from tomatoes, peaches, or pears easier by dipping into them boiling water before peeling.

- Oven-baked potatoes bake quicker if you first boil them in salted water for 10 minutes before placing in the pre-heated oven.

- To prevent splattering when pan frying, sprinkle salt in the pan.

- When frying chicken, flour the chicken and then refrigerate it for an hour or so. The coating sticks better.

- When browning meats, make sure the meat is dry and the pan and oil are very hot.

Kitchen Measurement Conversions

Kitchen measurement conversions are essential for getting it perfectly right in the kitchen. But, actual measurements are rarely used in traditional Nigerian cooking. Experienced cooks (the grandmothers, aunts, and mothers) have an expert feel of what requires a little dash of what where and when. No actual measurements needed! However, modern cooks (the younger generations) need accurate measurement guides. The kitchen measurement conversions below are useful for that purpose.

1 pinch	1/8 tea spoon or less
3 tea spoons	1 table spoon
2 table spoons	1/8 cup
4 table spoons	1/4 cup
8 table spoons	1/2 cup
12 table spoons	3/4 cup
16 table spoons	1 cup
4 oz	1/2 cup
8 oz	1 cup
16 oz	1 lb
1 oz	2 table spoons fat or liquid
1 cup of liquid	1/2 pint
2 cups	1 pint
2 pints	1 quart
4 cups of liquid	1 quart

1 quarts	1 gallon
1 jigger	1 ½ fluid oz
1 jigger	3 table spoons

Keeping Hot Soup Hot

Have you ever wondered why Chinese soups stay hot longer than those you cook at home? The secret is usually in the pepper oil, which makes the soup not only spicy hot but also temperature hot because it acts as an insulator on the surface of the soup. Any edible additive that can insulate the surface of soup will help to keep it hot longer. In addition, ingredients (i.e., solute) that lower the freezing point of soup (as with water) will also lower the cooling point of the soup.

Culinary Creativity

Eggs are exactly (eggxactly) right for many recipes. Eggs play an important recipe role in virtually all cultures around the world. Nigeria is not an exemption. Raw, parboiled, or hardboiled, eggs can feature in breakfast, lunch, or dinner recipes. Hardboiled eggs placed in meat stews in Nigeria is particularly a desirable sign of culinary sophistication. We often practice this in our own kitchen.

In the pre-television days, the fascination with eggs could be seen in neighborhood games among youths in Nigeria, whereby kids go around the neighborhood with their hardboiled eggs to compete in end-to-end egg smashing games. This is usually done with guinea fowl eggs, which are already harder shelled than regular chicken eggs. The sharper end of the egg (rather than the blunt end) is used for the game. The winning egg is the one that does not crack when smashed against another egg. The owner of the un-smashed wins (and collects) the smashed egg. Through this game, a lucky game could amass a larger collection of smashed eggs in a day, to be consumed and shared later on as a bounty of the competition. Fun were those egg-smashing days in Nigeria.

Embracing physics in the kitchen facilitates all kinds of culinary creativity. Nigerians are particularly innovative in the kitchen by coming up with new gastronomical experimentations, such as hard-boiled eggs in pepper stews.

Egg-washing is an example of using eggs for alternate uses for culinary creativity. Egg wash consists of a mixture of various ingredients that are combined to be brushed on the surface of breads and rolls before baking in order to give the crust an added brownness, crispness and/or sheen after the item is baked. Depending on the ingredients added to the mixture, an egg wash can provide a variety of different appearances to the surface of baked goods. The basic egg wash is a simple mixture of egg and water stirred or beaten together. Milk is also often used for the mixture. Below is a general guide for applying egg wash options:

- Whole egg and salt - provides a shiny surface

- Whole egg and milk - provides a medium shiny surface

- Whole egg and water - provides a golden amber colored surface

- Egg yolk and water - provides a shiny surface with a golden amber color

- Egg yolk and cream - provides a shiny surface with a darker brown color

- Egg white - provides a crispy surface with a lighter coloring

Human Evolution and Advancement of Food

Food origin is the very origin of Mankind. "Biology determines what we are, Chemistry explains what makes us what we are, and Physics describes what we do," so we claim, based on our direct culinary experiences. Food is an essential dimension of our existence. The original quote above is a manifestation of the biology, chemistry, and physics engendered in all manners of food preparation over the millennia. The history of food preparation goes back to the very beginning of man and woman. Since the dawn of time, human beings have taken delight in the science and art of cooking and eating. Culinary expertise and gastronomic interests are continually combined to satisfy our ever increasingly sophisticated palate. We tickle our palate with new food experiences and experimentations. A person's food preferences are shaped by several factors including the following:

- Country of origin

- Personal health consciousness

- Religion

- Economic order

- Cultural affiliation

- Ethnic origin

- Social class

- Language cluster

- Family group

- Community setting

- Residential locality

- Caste system

- Professional genre

- Educational awareness

- Acquired taste due to repeated trial, experimentation, or "force-feeding"

We strongly believe that food experimentation helps build a stomach that tolerates different cuisines.

By the Grace of Rice

Like garri, rice is another popular player in the kitchen physics of Nigeria. The quote below bears this out cogently:

"Rice is born in water and must die in wine." - Italian Proverb

Food, particularly rice, has played a significant role in the development of society and order of the day as evidenced by the facts below. In the early days, temples were used as banks and the first loans were taken out against rice. Where there is rice, there is less hunger. Rice, in all its glory, adorns dinner tables in all corners of the world. It is one of the most versatile and ubiquitous foods on the more people around the world than any other single food item. It has, thus, been used effectively to combat hunger in impoverish parts of the world. Rice has been studied as much intellectually as it has been passed around the table. In 2005, an international news brief announced that scientists have cracked the DNA code of rice. A team of scientists from ten countries reportedly teamed up to decipher the genetic code of rice. This scientific advancement is expected to speed up attempts to improve rice as a food crop that feeds most of the world's population. Rice is the first crop plant to have its genome sequenced. This means that scientists have identified virtually all the 389 million chemical building blocks of rice's DNA. Farmers and breeders can use this information to produce new rice varieties to satisfied specific gastronomic needs. For example, higher yield, more nutritional values, and better resistance to disease and pests are possible. This will ensure that rice will continue to enjoy its royal place in kitchens around the world for generations to come. The various "seductions of rice" are profiled in the excellent book by Jeffrey Alford and Naomi Duguid entitled "Seductions of Rice: A Cookbook" (Artisan/Workman Publishing, Inc., NY, 1998).

Deji's Ode to Rice

Rice comes in a variety of colorful and enticing bags in all sizes. This is aptly said by the Tsuji quote below.

"Rice is a beautiful food. It is beautiful when it grows, precision rows of sparkling green stalks shooting up to reach the hot summer sun. It is beautiful when harvested, autumn gold sheaves piled on diked, patchwork paddies. It is beautiful when, once threshed, it enters granary bins like a (flood) of tiny seed-pearls. It is beautiful when cooked by a practiced hand, pure white and sweetly fragrant." - Shizuo Tsuji

Like ice cream parfait, we could have rice parfait too. One of Deji's most-cherish gifts is a rice cookbook presented to him by his staff at the University of Tennessee, Knoxville on the occasion of Bosses Day in October 2004. Below is the signed inscription in the inside front cover of the book, "Seductions of Rice: A Cookbook" by Jeffrey Alford and Naomi Duguid (Artisan/Workman Publishing, Inc., New York, NY, 1998). It tells the story of his love affair with rice. Versatile rice goes with almost every other type of foods

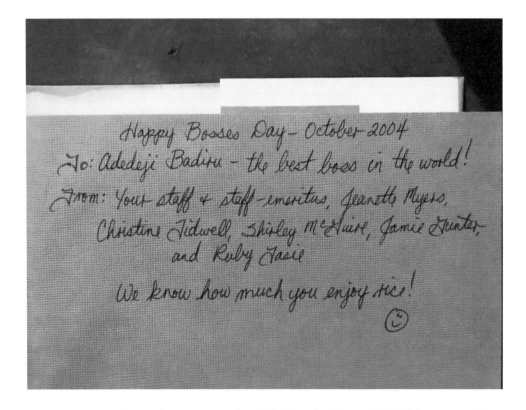

Deji's Ode to Rice

Rice, in my hot water, you rise magically.
You are the rice of my soul.
You are the rise of my day.
You are the apple of my eye.
When I see you, I salivate.
I live for you, you grow for me.
What a nice partnership that is!
You make me rise every morning;
You are the springboard of my day;
Each day, I rise to relish my rice;
The anchor of my recipe;
The root of my existence;
Without you, I am nothing but jelly;
I dream of you when I miss you on my plate;
Yes, you are my soul mate;
You are the very rice of my soul.
May you always rest in perfect harmony with my plate!

© 2014 Adedeji Badiru, ABICS Publications

==============================

Wild Rice Salad with Cashews

Rice is good. Cashews are good. Salad is definitely good and desirable. Why not combine all three for a really healthy meal? The recipe below does just that:

Ingredients:

1 cup uncooked wild rice

4 cups chicken broth

3 tablespoons of olive oil

1½ cup cashews, coarsely chopped

2 green onions, sliced

Dressing:

3 tablespoons of seasoned rice vinegar or apple cider vinegar

2 tablespoons of olive oil

1 tablespoons Asian sesame oil

1 clove garlic, minced

¼ tablespoon salt

A dash of freshly ground pepper

Instructions:

1. In a strainer, rinse wild rice under cool running water. Drain well.

2. In a 3-quart saucepan, bring rice and chicken broth to a boil over high heat

3. Reduce heat and simmer, covered, for 45 minutes or until rice is tender. Drain excess liquid and set rice aside.

4. In a medium skillet, heat 3 tablespoons oil over medium heat. Add peppers and cook for 5 minutes or until tender.

5. Add cashews and green onions. Cook for 2 to 3 minutes or until nuts begin to brown. Remove from heat. In a large bowl, stir wild rice with bell pepper mixture.

6. For dressing, combine vinegar, oils, garlic, salt, and pepper in a jar with a tight-fitting lid. Shake well. Pour dressing over salad and toss to coat the salad. Cover and refrigerate for at least two hours.

7. Enjoy!

Evolution of Kitchen Gadgets

The creativity of product developers has resulted in new kitchen gadgets in recent years. Although functional knives have existed for ages, the market is now replete with new introductions of knives of various shapes, colors, sizes, and advertised functionalities. Newly-introduced kitchen gadgets entice and lead users to overzealous, overuse, and over-dependent applications. Most new kitchen knives are nothing more than novelties. Once the novelty wears off, buyers resort to the age-old proven old reliable, the basic kitchen knives. Rather than collecting the over-abundance of new kitchen gadgets, a good cook will find out that many basic kitchen tools are versatile enough to meet a variety of improvised uses in the kitchen. There is no need to acquire new-improved gadgets with new dedicated applications. But, it can be fun and satisfying just to have the variety of "modern" gadgets in your kitchen. We, the authors here, also have fallen for the novelty-purchased kitchen knives. From the traditional grinding stones, electric blenders and modern food processors to revolutionary infrared kitchen aids, humans have devised and developed tools dedicated to the pursuit of cooking.

Grinding stones have played a special role in the history of mankind. In ancient times, Neolithic and Upper Paleolithic people used millstone to grind grains, nuts, rhizomes and other vegetable food products for consumption. These implements are often called grinding stones. They used either saddlestones or rotary querns turned by hand. Such devices were also used to grind pigments and metal ores prior to smelting. Various uses have been documented over the centuries. Millstones are used in windmills and watermills, including tide mills, for grinding wheat or other grains. In old-time Britain millstones were used for grinding barley. In France, burrstones were used for finer grinding. In India, grinding stones (*Chakki*) were used to grind grains and spices. These consist of a stationary stone cylinder upon which a smaller stone cylinder rotates. Smaller ones, for household use, were operated by two people. Larger ones, for community or commercial use, used livestock to rotate the upper cylinder.

Until recent years, grinding stones were a big part of the Nigerian kitchen. Women have used it for grinding of grains and spices. It is quite possible that some indigenous villagers still use grinding stones. Expert users claim they like grinding stones because of the preciseness they can get, in spite of the laborious process. To grind, women would use a piece of stone in a cylindrical shape in both hand. She would put grains on the surface of the base stone and would run the smaller stone over the grain using all her might. She would move the implement back and forth across the surface of the grinding until the grains are well grinded to the level of fineness desired. In the Nigerian Yoruba language, the base stone is called "**ọlọ**," which literally means grinder. The smaller hand-held stone is called "**ọmọ ọlọ**," which literally means "child of the grinder." Of course, "mother" and "child" must go together in other to get the grinding job done. Using "child" this way in the Yoruba vernacular makes references to the smaller or lesser member of a partnership or pairing of implements. In our present modern times, technology and science have since changed the way spices and ingredients are manipulated in the kitchen. The indigenous Nigerian grinder shown below is used for grinding pepper, corn, egusi, and other local ingredients.

Corn is a very versatile crop that is converted to various forms for consumption or other uses ranging from animal feed, cosmetics, and ethanol fuel to thickener. Some industrial uses of corn include filler for plastics, packing materials, insulating materials, adhesives, chemicals, explosives, paint, paste, abrasives, dyes, insecticides, pharmaceuticals, organic acids, solvents, rayon, antifreeze, and soaps.

Ethnicity and Food Habits

Food habits are greatly influenced by ethnicity. Contrary to how some people view it, ethnicity is not the same as race. Ethnicity refers to the group to which an individual belongs based on cultural affiliation, language, food habits, social interests, religion, and family patterns. Race generally refers to the biological division to which an individual belongs based on color of skin, color and texture of hair, physical features, and other bodily characteristics. Because of intermarriage and evolution of time, race is sometimes viewed as a social construct and not amenable to strict demarcation lines. The lines of food demarcation are very fuzzy. Over the generations, food practices and recipes have cross-fertilized and morphed into hybrids of recipes and customized variations to fit the consumer's tastes and preferences.

Benefits to Body, Mind, and Soul

Body and soul benefit from the products of the Nigerian kitchen. Of the body, eating provides nourishments that are essential for life, healing, and thriving as a social being.

Of the soul, eating offers pleasure that excites the senses that makes a person what he or she is spiritually and socially. While the body represents the engagement of time and space, it is the soul that creates the aura that ties everything together. Essentially, the soul is the atmosphere, spiritual or otherwise, within which the body resides.

Of the mind, eating expands the mind both through the anticipatory comfort of the food as well as the gratification of going through the action of consumption. A dull mind can result from not being exposed to a wide variety of food. The quote below summarizes the essentials of culinary physics:

"...all the charming and beautiful things, from the Song of Songs, to bouillabaisse, and from the nine Beethoven symphonies to the Martini cocktail, have been given to humanity by men who, when the hour came, turned from tap water to something with color in it, and more in it than mere oxygen and hydrogen." - H.L. Mencken

KITCHEN MOLECULAR MOVEMENTS

What is physics? True to the title of this book, "Kitchen Physics," this chapter presents a brief account of physics in the context of what happens in the kitchen. Physics is the branch of science that tells us what we can and cannot do. It is the science of our actions. In the context of this book, that is kitchen actions. In other words, physics is the science of our actions. As long as we perform actions in the kitchen, physics is, indeed, applicable in our kitchen. The quote below aptly describes the connectivity.

"What yeast has wrought, let heat manifest. Heat and steam provide the beat; all the meat has to do is dance in the pot." - Deji Badiru (From "Physics in the Nigerian Kitchen," 2010)

"Biology determines what we are, Chemistry explains what makes us what we are, and Physics describes what we do." - Deji Badiru (From "The Physics of Soccer," 2010)

The website, www.physicsofsoccer.com, presents a basic framework for applying physics in many of our day-to-day activities. For example, Newton's Laws of Motion are echoed below.

Newton's First Law of Motion:

An object at rest tends to stay at rest and an object in motion tends to stay in motion with the same speed and in the same direction unless acted upon by an unbalanced force.

The first law is, perhaps, the most readily observable in the kitchen and elsewhere. A person already in motion will more easily continue to be in motion and be able to "spring" into action in response to events in the kitchen. A person who is stationary will have a more difficult time responding to mobile events in the kitchen. For general health and fitness purposes, being in frequent motion (rather than sedentary practices) is essential for building a healthy lifestyle, in combination with a healthy diet. If you sit around, your body will accommodate sitting around. If you stay active, your body will embrace and accept active lifestyles. So, under the First Law, you may ask "what makes a tick tick?" The "flow of blood," one might say. Below are the three Laws of Motion postulated and proven by Sir Isac Newton (1642 – 1727).

<u>Newton's Second Law of Motion:</u>

The acceleration of an object as produced by a net force is directly proportional to the magnitude of the net force, in the same direction as the net force, and inversely proportional to the mass of the object. This is represented in equation form as Force = Mass times Acceleration. In a kitchen analogy, an action taken in the direction of the intended placement of an item requires effort (force) to be applied by the actor. Jettisoning a soiled kitchen utensil from across the kitchen into the sink is a good example that readers can imagine.

<u>Newton's Third Law of Motion:</u>

Newton's Third Law of Motion states that for every action there is an equal and opposite reaction. A force is a push or a pull upon an object that results from its interaction with another object. Forces result from interactions between objects. According to Newton, whenever objects A and B interact with each other, they exert forces upon each other. When a cook sits in a kitchen chair, his or her body exerts a downward force on the chair, and the chair exerts an upward force on his or her body. There are two forces resulting from this interaction: a force on the chair and a force on the body. These two forces are called *action* and *reaction* forces in Newton's third law of motion. One key thing to remember is that inanimate objects, such as walls, can push and pull back on an object, such as a soccer ball. For a manifestation of this law, think of actions and reactions in a kitchen.

The Thermodynamics of Food Preparation

Cooking is all about the science of physics and chemistry. Over the centuries, humans have learned how to exploit the natural phenomenon of energy transfer through heat for the purpose of transforming food from one form (usually raw) to another form (usually cooked) to facilitate the experience of food consumption.

Thermodynamics is the science of heat transfer between two objects. Heat and steam provide the beat, to which molecules of ingredients dance to create gastronomical delights for dining tables around the world. . . . . Like the opening quote above indicates, Biology, Chemistry, and Physics play direct and intertwining roles in our existence and activities, including gastronomic pursuits. To galvanize ingredients to create a marvel for the palate is, indeed, a testimony to the inner workings of science, fueled by fire, steam, and molecules. The transformation from solid to liquid to vapor makes physics in the kitchen fun and gratifying.

Food is primarily composed of water, fat, protein, carbohydrates, and, unfortunately, impurities. Cooking is the process of transferring energy, usually heat, from an energy source to the food long enough to change its chemistry to achieve a desired level of flavor, texture, tenderness, juiciness, appearance, and nutrition while ensuring safety and digestibility.

Modes of Heat Transfer

Food preparation, whichever way we slice it, requires heat transfer from one source to the other. The heat-source-and-sink relationship has been the keystone of food preparation for centuries. Modern processes have advanced and simplified the heat-source-to-food interface. It is through an appropriate use of heat that food undergoes metamorphosis from one form to another. Intermediate stages of this metamorphosis can their own rights in terms of food texture, aroma, flavor, and taste. There are five primary modes of heat transfer:

1. Induction

2. Radiation

3. Convection

4. Conduction

5. Excitation

Whether indoor cooking or outdoor cooking, heat transfer is still the primary physics of getting our foods ready for consumption. In communal ethnic village kitchens around the world, the locals have understood the practical principles of utilizing heat transfer in its various forms for a long time, well before written guidance came along.

Induction heating is the process of heating an electrically conducting object (usually a metal) by electromagnetic induction, where currents are generated within the metal and resistance leads to heating of the metal. An induction heater consists of an electromagnet, through which a high-frequency alternating current (AC) is passed. Heat may also be generated by magnetic *hysteresis*, a phenomenon in which magnetic materials show a resistance to any fast-paced changes in their magnet level. This resistance creates friction, which contributes to the cooking heat. The frequency of AC used depends on the object size, material type, coupling (between the work coil and the object to be heated) and the penetration depth. Some modern rice cookers take advantage of the science and technology of induction heating. While other rice cookers apply heat directly from an electrical plate underneath the inner cooking pan, induction-heating rice cookers get their heat from an alternating electric current from the electric power source. Induction heating, used for many applications beyond rice cookers, is achieved when the current passes through metal coils, typically made of copper. The movement of the current through these coils creates a magnetic field. It is into this magnetic field that the rice cooker's pan is inserted. The magnetic field produces an electrical current inside the cooking pan, and this generates heat. Induction heating improves rice cookers in three main ways:

- The temperature-sensing methods can be more accurate, allowing for fine-tuned adjustments in temperature.

- The heat distribution area can encompass the inner cooking pan, not just radiate upwards from below, to produce more evenly cooked food.

- The level of heat being created in the cooking pan can be changed in an instant by strengthening or weakening the magnetic field that is generating it.

Induction is the latest technology used in stove tops. A copper coil is placed under a smooth cooktop and an alternating current is sent through the coil creating a rapidly changing electromagnetic field. Electrons in conductive steel or cast iron pots placed above the electromagnet are jostled by the rapidly changing magnetism. The electrons exhibit resistance, which gets them to become hot. The pot then conducts the heat to the food without the cooktop or the air around it getting hot. Induction is very responsive to the control knob of the stove and it is extremely energy efficient, but it does not work well with aluminum, glass, or copper pots. This is often baffling to homeowners who complain that certain pots don't cook as fast as others in their kitchen. Lesson to remember: Aluminum, glass, and copper don't conduct heat very well for induction cooking purposes.

Radiation heating is the transfer of heat by direct exposure (without actual touching) to a source of energy. Grilling a hamburger directly over hot coals is cooking mostly with radiant heat with the exception of the parts touching the hot grates. Radiation heating is the reason that nuclear bombs are so destructive.

Convection heating is when heat is carried to the food by a fluid such as air, water, or oil. Cooking a sausage on kitchen oven, where it is surrounded by hot oil, is convection heating. Hot oil, as a medium of convection heat transfer is more effective than using hot air because oil is denser than air and it packs more heat per inch than air. Deep frying a turkey is convection heating. However, the interior of the turkey is cooked by conduction as the heat travels through it without it directly touching the hot oil.

Conduction heating occurs when heat is transferred to the food by contact with the heat source. For example, cooking a sausage in a frying pan is conduction heating. Conduction happens as the surface of the meat gets hotter than the interior and the heat transfers to the center through the moisture and fats. As with most natural processes, heat flows from a region of high concentration to a region of lower concentration. The grill marks on food are caused by conduction heating due to actual touching of the food with the heated surface.

Excitation heating is how microwave ovens work. Microwaves are radio waves that penetrate the food and vibrate the molecules *inside* the food until it gets hot without heating the air around it. Water heats first in the microwave. Technically, this can also be viewed as a form of radiant heat cooking because the molecules get excited, agitated, and highly mobile due to the radiant impact of radio waves.

Traditional cooking in Africa takes advantage of all the different forms of heat transfer described above, albeit in their local and unrefined forms. While the indigenous cooking approaches might not have been recognized in their scientific names, as enumerated above, they are, nonetheless, inherently scientific in their impacts and outputs. The physics of cooking is the same all over the world. The Appalachian (USA) outdoor cooking scenes in the frontier days are very much like the village cooking scenes in Africa.

Common Food Preparation Methods

If you cook by the wrong method, a tender cut of meat can turn out tough and undesirable.

If you cook by the right method, a tough cut of meat can turn out tender. It is in the science!

We have a multitude of options for cooking our foods. We cannot complain . . . or we should not. Below are the common methods of cooking. Permutations and combinations of the methods are often used to achieve specific cooking objectives. Each method, or combinations thereof, has its own unique physics and chemistry impacts on the food. The interplay of temperature and pressure plays a significant role in cooking.

Au gratin: In this cooking, the dish if topped with buttered crumbs or cheesy crumbs that have been oven-browned.

Baking: This is cooking with dry heat in an enclosed contraption such as an oven or in a large covered pot.

Barbecue (Barbeque, BBQ, Bar-B-Q, Bar-B-Que, Bar-B-Cue, 'Cue, 'Que, Barbie): Barbecue is the oldest cooking method and has been practiced in Africa, Europe, and Asia since the beginning of humans. It involves throwing meat onto hot coals or hanging it above the hot coals. The options for fueling the barbecue heat include wood, charcoal, wood pellets, and gas.

The key to a great barbecue is to cook the meat using low indirect heat for a long period of time to allow the meat to become tender and moist. The OinkADoodleMoo BBQ that the first author patronizes in Dayton, Ohio prides itself on cooking barbecue for 18 hours slowly. They will not sell any barbecue cooked for less than that. Generally, the temperature of the barbecuing heat should range from 200 to 300 degrees Fahrenheit.

Bisque: This is usually a thick, creamy soup. This term can also be used for a frozen cream dessert.

Blanching: In this, foods are submerged in boiling water for a very short time, usually less than five minutes, and then they are usually moved to cold water. The process is used to partially cook a food, to loosen skins on nuts to make them easy to remove, or to make green vegetables become bright green.

Boiling: This is cooking by submerging in boiling water. The bubbles in the boiling water are steam rising to the surface of the hot water. Water boils at 212°F (100°C) at sea level and once it hits that temp it does not rise any higher, no matter how much heat is applied. Boiling temperatures decrease as you go up in altitude because the column of air on top of the liquid is shorter and exerting less pressure so it is easier for water vapor, in the form of steam, to escape. In a high-altitude location, water will boil at some lower temperature. For example, in Denver, the boiling temp of water is about 203°F. We cannot make liquids boil faster by increasing the heat. Boiling is a very severe method of cooking and can easily damage food by breaking down its structure and squeezing out its moisture. Thus, boiled meat can become dry, particularly if aired out after the boiling process.

Braising: This is a wet method of cooking similar to stewing, poaching, or simmering, but the food is usually not submerged as they are in those methods. It is only partially covered in hot, but not boiling liquid for a long time, perhaps 6 to 12 hours. Braising is usually done in large pots, such as Dutch ovens and slow cookers, with the lid not on tight. This keeps the food in the air cooler than the 212°F of the liquid, and allows it to tenderize without drying out as easily.

Broasting®: This is a trademarked method of cooking chicken and other foods using a pressure fryer and condiments. The technique was invented and marketed by the **Broaster Company** of Beloit, Wisconsin. Broasting equipment and ingredients are marketed only to food service and institutional customers, including supermarkets and fast food restaurants. They are not available to the general public. The method essentially combines pressure cooking with deep frying chicken that has been marinated and breaded. The resulting chicken is said to be crisp on the outside and moist on the inside, i.e., like traditional fried chicken but less greasy. Another advantage of broasting over deep-frying is that large quantities of chicken can be prepared more quickly, 12–13 minutes instead of 20.

Broiling: This is direct heat cooking with flame. It is similar to grilling. In recent years the meaning has been confused, and many people refer to broiling as when the flame is directly above the food, but technically it can be either above or below.

Char broiling: This is broiling over charcoal. The grill manufacturer, Char-Broil, makes more gas grills than charcoal grills.

Curing: This is like cooking, but not quite. Although heat is not necessary to cure meats (actually usually done at cool temps), curing is like cooking in that it changes the chemistry of the meat. Curing involves the preservation of meat by the heavy application of some or all of the following: Salts, sugars, nitrates, nitrites, or smoke. Each works differently by altering meat chemistry, inhibiting some microbial growth while promoting others, altering enzymatic digestion, changing the color, and of course, flavoring the meat.

Deep frying: This is cooking at a high temperature, usually 350 to 360°F, by submerging in oil or fat. This method creates more heat than boiling. The high heat creates steam within the food which cooks it and creates pressure at the interface between the food and oil preventing the oil from penetrating if the temperature is properly set. Deep fried foods are usually crisp on the exterior and moist in the interior. Because deep fried foods are often dipped in starch or batter, they can be extra crispy. However, the batter can absorb significant oil, which may not be healthy eating.

Drying: This is the process of dehydrating food by warming it slightly in a low humidity, high airflow environment. It is an excellent method of food preservation since most microbes need water to thrive.

Frappe: This is a food preparation in which the food is lightly frozen.

F**reeze drying**: This is done by freezing the food in a low-pressure environment, and then a small amount of heat is applied to sublimate (evacuate, evaporate, remove) the moisture.

Grilling: This is cooking with direct heat over flame or directly over a heat source. Grilling is usually hot and fast cooking. Grilling is usually done between 350 to 550 degrees Fahrenheit, using either propane gas or charcoal. Meat can be grilled either "directly" or "indirectly." This refers to the proximity of the meat to the heat source. Indirect grilling ensures a more gradual and even cook.

Microwave Cooking: This is a fast and convenient method of cooking, whereby excitation of molecules in the food is accomplished through microwaves. Molecules deep inside the food vibrate and heat up without heating the air around it. The effect is similar to steaming. There is no dry heat to create the Maillard effect, which is the flavorful crusting of the meat surface. As the surface of foods heat above 310°F, a reaction of amino acids and sugars occur, forming a multitude of new compounds (i.e., organic chemistry), and the surfaces start to brown. This is the Maillard reaction. It creates a richness and depth of flavor and a crunchy texture. It is through the Maillard effect that steaks get grill marks, roasts develop a bark, bread loaves form crusts, slices of bread turn golden in the toaster, coffee beans turn dark when roasted, and fried potatoes darken. The sugar compounds formed also begin to caramelize, producing an appealing appearance of the food.

Pan Roasting: In this method of cooking, the cook starts with a piece of meat, often a thick piece of fish, by browning and crisping the exterior in a thin layer of hot oil in a frying pan. But the meat is still uncooked in the center. The cook then puts the pan in the oven to finish cooking. The result is food that is fried on the top and bottom and baked in the center.

Planking: This is a combination method of indirect cooking, especially popular with salmon. A wood plank, usually untreated western red cedar, which is porous and aromatic, is soaked in water. The food is placed on top of the plank and the plank is placed over direct heat in a closed oven. The plank heats the food by conduction, the water creates steam, the underside of the plank burns creating smoke, and the food roasts in the closed environment. Thus, we have a combination of conduction, steaming, smoking and roasting. Note that construction woods should never be used for planking because they can be treated with toxic chemicals as preservatives.

Poaching: This is similar to stewing, but poaching is usually done in water, or water with just a little salt and/or vinegar added.

Pressure Cooking: Pressure cookers are heavy sealed pots with a locking lid and a high-pressure release valve. A small amount of moisture is placed with the food in the cooker. As the pot heats up, moisture and pressure build up. The boiling point of water rises as pressure builds. So, the food cooks at a higher temp and, thus, faster than when steaming under normal pressure. The resulting food resembles braised or simmered food.

Roasting: Traditionally, this is a method of cooking in the open in front of an open flame. Nowadays, it is often done in an enclosed oven with medium to high heat, such as in baking. Customarily, the food is exposed to heat only on one side at a time. But, nowadays, the food is usually surrounded by dry heat and it browns with the Maillard effect and caramelizes evenly. Food can be roasted on a grate, in a pan, on a skewer, or other food holders.

Roux: This refers to butter and flour cooked into a paste to thicken sauces.

Rotisserie: This is a form or roasting where the food rotates in front of or above a flame so that the meat gets hot on one side and then cools and gets hot again, in an iterative process. Some of the heat is absorbed into the food and some dissipates in the air. The interior cooks evenly.

Sautéing: This is a method of cooking food in a small amount of fat or oil over a high heat on a hot metal surface, usually in a frying pan or skillet, with the goal of rapid cooking and browning. This method helps the food retain moisture and helps prevent it from absorbing oil. To be successful it is important the food is not too cold, the surface of the food must be dry, and the pan cannot be crowded. Sautéing onions and garlic reduces their bite and pungency, and converts some of the compounds to sugar giving them a form of sweetness.

Simmering: This is a slow cooking process under low heat. It is usually done after a period of high-heat cooking.

Smoking: This is a way to cook, flavor, or preserve food by exposing it to smoke, usually from wood, corncobs, tea, and herbs. In the days before refrigeration, smoking was a widely used method of food preservation. But it is not good for all foods since smoke does not penetrate very far into the food. **Cold smoking** is usually done at temperatures under 125°F. The food is heavily infused with smoke flavor, but it is not cooked by heat. This method requires specialize expertise to do it right. Unless done properly, microbes can thrive in the low-temperature of cold smoking, thus increasing the risk of food that is dangerous. For this reason, cold smoked meats are often heavily salted, brined, or otherwise cured. Cold smoking of meats should not be done at home. It should be done professionally. Most commercial smoked fishes and cheeses are cold smoked. **Hot smoking** is usually done at temperatures in the 165 to 200°F range. These foods are often also brined or cured. Most American smoked hams are hot smoked. **Smoke roasting** is usually done in the vicinity of 200 to 250°F. The food is cooked by the heat, and when it is finished it is free of harmful living microbes. At these temperatures, not much shrinkage occurs. Smoke roasting is relatively easy to do on backyard smokers and barbecue equipment. Most of the best barbecued ribs, pulled pork, and briskets are done with smoke roasting.

Sous-vide: This is French for "under vacuum" and it means putting the meat in a vacuum sealed plastic bag and immersing it in water at the desired serving temperature for hours, even days! It is similar to poaching but more flexible. The process also prevents liquids from escaping, and some chefs add butter or sauce to the bag to build more flavor. Meats come out uniform in color and texture throughout, so they are sometimes seared after cooking to create a Maillard effect crust. Sous-vide must be done correctly because possesses a deadly risk of developing botulism.

Steaming: In steaming, the food is placed in an enclosed container above boiling water. Steam penetrates the food. It is a very effective method of tenderizing and moisturizing and it is fast. Crabs are often the beneficiaries of this type of cooking.

Stewing: In this method of preparation, food is cooked under a water-based liquid at medium temperatures, usually between 160 to 211°F. Stewing usually is a slow cooking process. Stewed meats are usually browned by sautéing or broiling first to add flavor. These methods can be done in a pot over a heat source or in a slow cooker. The liquids are usually flavored with stock, wine, vegetables, herbs, etc. Ethnic African and Asian stews are famous for their variety, taste, and invigorating aromas.

Stir frying: This is similar to sautéing, but the food is cooked in a curved pan called a wok, and the food is often not browned. Stir frying is often done with a toss of various ingredients, all dancing to the tune of aromatic interactions and enmeshing while the pan stirs.

Surface frying: This method of cooking is frying in a thin layer of oil on a hot metal surface, much like sautéing, but usually on a griddle. Only one surface at a time fries as opposed to deep frying. Specialty burgers are usually prepared this way.

Sweating: Sweating is like sautéing, but done at much lower temperatures. Food is placed in a pot or pan with enough fat or oil to coat it but cooked at low temperatures until it softens or wilts. In other words, the food sweats out its internal moisture.

Infrared Cooking

Infrared (**IR**) light is electromagnetic radiation with longer wavelengths than those of visible light. The infrared range of wavelengths corresponds to a frequency range that includes most of the thermal radiation emitted by objects near room temperature. Infrared light is emitted or absorbed by molecules when they change their rotational-vibrational movements. Much of the energy from the Sun arrives on Earth in the form of infrared radiation. Out of the energy of the sun reaching the Earth, portions are in infrared radiation, visible light, and ultraviolet radiation. Infrared light is used in industrial, scientific, medical, and more recently, cooking applications. Night-vision devices using infrared illumination allow people or animals to be observed without the observer being detected. In astronomy, imaging at infrared wavelengths allows observation of objects obscured by interstellar dust. Infrared imaging cameras are used to detect heat loss in insulated systems, observe changing blood flow in the skin, and overheating of electrical apparatus.

Infrared is energy radiation with a frequency below the sensitivity of our eyes. So, we cannot see an infrared wave, but we can very well feel it as heat on our skin. With so much energy, infrared is well suited for cooking purposes albeit with a proper design and control of the cooking apparatus. Infrared rays penetrate the food to provide the cooking effect.

French Appreciation of Foie Gras

Many people consider Foie Gras tabu. **Foie gras,** which is French for "fat liver" is a food product made of the liver of a duck or goose that has been specially fattened through corn force-feeding, which is known as gavage. Foie gras is a popular and well-known delicacy in French cuisine. Its flavor is described as rich, buttery, and delicate, unlike that of an ordinary duck or goose liver. Foie gras is sold whole, or is prepared into mousse, parfait, or pastry and may also be served as an accompaniment to another food item, such as steak. French law states that "Foie gras belongs to the protected cultural and gastronomical heritage of France." The technique of gavage is said to date as far back as 2500 BC, when the ancient Egyptians began keeping birds for food and deliberately fattened the birds through force-feeding. Today, France is by far the largest producer and consumer of foie gras, though it is produced and consumed worldwide, particularly in other European nations, the United States, and China. Gavage-based foie gras production is controversial due to the force-feeding procedure used. A number of countries and other jurisdictions have laws against force feeding or the sale of foie gras.

The French appreciation of foie gras is a testimony that foods that border on being gross and unpleasant in one culture may, indeed, be coveted delicacies in another culture. Examples of such foods abound in most African and Asian cuisine. These include goat intestines, chicken feet, sheep brains, beef tongue, bull testicles, snake gallbladder, fermented cod fish (stockfish), and so on.

Molecular Gastronomy

Molecular gastronomy is a scientific discipline that studies the physical and chemical processes that occur while cooking. Molecular gastronomy seeks to investigate and explain the chemical reasons behind the transformation of ingredients, as well as the social, artistic and technical components of culinary and gastronomic phenomena in general. For example, molecular gastronomy includes the study of how different cooking temperatures affect food. Talking about artistic rendition, food looks much better and appetizing when decorated artistically to appeal to all the senses of food appreciation.

There are many branches of food science, all of which study different aspects of food such as safety, microbiology, preservation, chemistry, engineering, physics and the like. Until the advent of molecular gastronomy, there was no formal scientific discipline dedicated to studying the processes in regular cooking as done in the home or in a restaurant. The aforementioned have mostly been concerned with industrial food production and while the disciplines may overlap with each other to varying degrees, they are considered separate areas of investigation.

Though many disparate examples of the scientific investigation of cooking exist throughout history, the creation of the discipline of molecular gastronomy was intended to bring together what had previously been fragmented and isolated investigation into the chemical and physical processes of cooking into an organized discipline within food science to address what the other disciplines within food science either do not cover, or cover in a manner intended for scientists rather than cooks.

Culinary Physics

Much of the culinary invention in recent decades has been a result of trial and error rather than rigorous scientific research. Serendipity is a common occurrence in cooking. Culinary physics explains the structure and characteristics of food. An example is the classic emulsion process, whereby a liquid is dispersed into another liquid. With a greater understanding of the physical parameters of food, we will know more about how to manipulate them to the extent of our gastronomic desires.

Measurement of Spiciness

Many ethnic cuisines are inherently spicy. But how do we measure how spicy a food is? There is a science for that! Almost all segments of the country indulge in spicy foods as it is believed that a tongue that can withstand the spice demonstrates the owner's path to a clear soul. Depending on the tasters resilience, hot spices can blur the line between pleasure and pain. So, how hot is spicy hot? The **Scoville scale** is a measurement of the spicy heat (a.k.a piquancy) of a pepper. The number of **Scoville heat units** indicates the amount of capsaicin present. Capsaicin is a chemical compound that stimulates chemoreceptor nerve endings in the skin, especially the mucous membranes. The scale is named after its creator, American chemist Wilbur Scoville, who developed a test for rating the pungency of chili peppers. His method, which he devised in 1912, is known as the Scoville Organoleptic Test. An alternative method for quantitative analysis uses high-performance liquid chromatography, making it possible to directly measure capsaicinoid content. Capsaicin is the main capsaicinoid in peppers. The wall chart below shows the degrees of spiciness.

Does water always Freeze at 32 degrees?

No. Although the freezing point of water is 32 degrees, there are cases where water does not freeze at that temperature. Sure, ordinary water freezes at 32 degrees. But one case of exception is "supercooling," in which case distilled or purified water may not freeze even below 32 degrees if it is placed undisturbed in the freezer. This is because the process of crystallizing, which is needed for freezing to occur, may not happen in pure water. Impurities, however tiny, and disturbance ripples are needed to initiate crystallization. If the supercooled water is moved, even out of the refrigerator, it immediately begins to freeze. How about that for the wonders of physics!

An Apple a Day Does What?

Can an Apple a day really keep the doctor away? No, not really. But, yes, to some extent. Read on. An apple a day keeping the doctor away is believed to have come from an ancient Roman proverb. The apple was believed to have magical powers to cure all kinds of illnesses. This is probably because of the proven properties of the

Fiber: Apples are a good source of dietary fiber. Typical measurements reveal about 4 grams of dietary fiber per five ounce apple. This equates to approximately 15% of the recommended daily intake. Apples contain both soluble and insoluble fiber in the form of cellulose and pectin. Both of these fibers have been documented to be beneficial for cholesterol.

Antioxidants and Vitamin C: Unlike animals, humans are unable to synthesize vitamin C in the body. It is, thus, essential to find a good natural source of vitamin C. Apples provide this source. Vitamin C is well known for preventing scurvy through the use of limes by the British Navy during 1795. It is also well known that vitamin C has many immune system enhancing properties and it is, therefore, important for overall health. Vitamin C is also a superb antioxidant, and it is essential for cell detoxification and enzymatic function. Apples also contain bioflavonoids, which are known for their antioxidant properties. Apples contain a long list of phytonutrients, including quercetin, catechin, phlorizin and chlorogenic acid. It is important to note that many of the nutrients of an apple are contained within the apple's skin. Thus, eating the skin is a good practice.

Antioxidants include vitamins A, C, and E as well as the mineral selenium. They are needed by the body for a variety of functions, including protecting against cancer, heart disease, cataracts, diabetes, and retinal failure, just to name a few. In ordinary language, antioxidants are substances or nutrients in foods, which can prevent or moderate the oxidative damage to the body. When cells in the body use oxygen, they naturally produce free radicals or by-products which can cause damage. Antioxidants possess the ability to prevent and repair damage done by free radicals. Common examples of antioxidants, by vitamin categories, are listed below:

Vitamin A: Carrots, squash, broccoli, sweet potatoes, tomatoes, kale, collards, cantaloupe, peaches, apricots, and bright-colored fruits and vegetables.

Vitamin C: Citrus fruits (oranges, lime), green peppers, broccoli, green leafy vegetables, strawberries, and tomatoes.

Vitamin E: Nuts, seeds, whole grains, green leafy vegetables, vegetable oil, and liver oil.

Selenium: Fish, shellfish, red meat, grains, eggs, chicken and garlic.

Other common sources of antioxidants include soy, red wine, purple grapes, concord grapes, cranberries, tea, tomato, pink grapefruit, watermelon, dark green vegetables, spinach, oatmeal, and barley.

Omega-3 Foods

Omega 3 are fatty acids derived from fish (e.g., fish oil), seaweed, flaxseed, and walnuts. Fish Oil is a natural source of Omega-3 fatty acids, which is vital for normal cell growth, and essential fatty acids play a key role in cell health. Omega-3 acids benefit the hearts of healthy people and those at high risk of cardiovascular disease. Salmon, flax seeds, soybeans, halibut, snapper, tofu, and walnuts are excellent food sources of Omega-3 fatty acids.

In a nutshell, Omega-3 fatty acids are healthy fats. For example, polyunsaturated fats, unlike saturated fats, are liquid at room temperature and remain liquid when refrigerated or frozen. Monounsaturated fats, found in olive oil, are liquid at room temperature, but harden when refrigerated. Each type of fat has health benefits depending on how it is prepared, used in recipes, and the amount consumed.

Food Homogeneity

Homogeneous foods exhibit uniform consistency of their properties, including color, texture, taste, and so on. Milk is a good example for explaining homogeneity. Raw milk is usually separated into its various natural components through centrifuge. The components are mixed in various proportions (combinations and permutations) to generate a host of products, such as butter, cream, skim milk, x% milk, and so on. The various milk types are homogenized to prevent their fatty solids from rising to the top of the milk. As every milk product, even skim milk, has some fat content, homogeneity makes it uniform in the final store-shelf properties.

Combinations and Permutations of Rice Dishes

Ingredient variations, combinations, and permutations rule in recipe world. Millions of people experiment with recipes and combinations and permutations of ingredients on a daily basis. Some hit the jackpot of new gastronomic discoveries while many have to go back to the drawing board . . . or shall we say, chopping board. With all these culinary experimentations, it is difficult for anyone to claim a patent on a recipe and expect to retain the rights for long. There are, however, proprietary recipes, such as Coca-Cola® and KFC® formulas. Other than secret proprietary formulas, recipes are one thing that everybody freely and proudly shares with others. Recipe sharing is the ingredient that can bind the world toward a better cultural understanding.

From basic shared recipes, new combinations and permutations evolve to generate new recipe creations. Consider a test question that requires students to compute the different number of meal choices possible, given a certain set of menu options. This is calculated by the combination and permutation formulas in Statistics. A typical question might ask for how many meal choices are able to a diner if, in a particular restaurant, there are three types of meat, four types of vegetables, five types of drinks, and six types of dessert. In this case, the answer is:

Meal choices   = 3(meat options) x 4(vegetable options) x 5(drink options) x 6(dessert options) = 360 unique meal choices

Isn't this amazing? So, when you complain of not having many menu options at a restaurant, you really haven't evaluated the number of combination options available. To extend the computational example further, consider the following. Suppose one and only one particular combination of meat option and drink option will kick in an allergic reaction for a diner, what is the probability that this particular diner can get sick at this particular restaurant if the meal options are selected at random? Using the laws of probability, the answer is calculated as Probability of allergic reaction = 1/360 = 0.002778. That is less than a 0.3 percent chance of this particular diner getting sick at this particular restaurant in a random combination of menu options. Of course, with prior knowledge of the allergic reaction tendencies of the diner, certain menu options can be eliminated from the initial set of options; thereby reducing the probability of getting sick to zero.

The above example can be made even more interesting by extending it to permutation, which is the number of possible arrangements of k objects selected from a pool of n objects. In that case, we may be looking at the order in which the menu options are consumed. For example, we can evaluate eating dessert before eating vegetables versus eating vegetables first. Each order represents a unique permutation. Analyses such as these can open up a whole new world of food for thought when evaluating meal options. Because this book is not about drawing statistical inferences about food options, we will leave further discussions to the imagination of the reader.

Science of Boiling Water

Salt in Water: Boiling water is a cornerstone of cooking rice. So, it helps to understand how water boils, from a scientific point of view. There are several myths and facts about boiling water. Water and salt are two of the most important essentials in a kitchen. It is interesting to note how they interact to do what we expect of them in terms of our food preparation. The effect of salt on the boiling point of water is particularly of interest, but only for theoretical reasons. For practical kitchen applications, the effect is negligible. But for scientific curiosity, we will examine the effect. Adding salt to water increases the boiling temperature (i.e., boiling point), causing the water to come to a boil more slowly. That is, it requires a higher temperature to boil. This increase in the cooking temperature will cause foods boiled in salt water to cook faster. Pure liquids (e.g., water) will generally have lower boiling points than mixtures (e.g., water and salt). For this reason, adding sugar to water has the same increasing effect on the boiling point as adding salt. If pure water is heated up to a high temperature prior to the addition of the salt, it could cause the entire pot to start boiling spontaneously. This is a result of the grains of salt acting as nucleation sites. This has the effect of making nearly-boiling water actually boil more quickly when salt is added. The tiny amount of salt required to cause a nucleation effect would have no effect on the temperature of the boiling water. In this regard, you can think of the salt as a catalyst, facilitating the change of state of the water from liquid to boiling.

Adding salt to water to raise the boiling point for cooking is actually negligible in practice. The amount of salt we normally add to water for typical cooking would have negligible effect on the boiling temperature. To easily remember this relationship, we present the visual plot below, based on a simple lab experiment. For fun experimentation purposes, you can add a few grains of salt to pure water to kick off the boiling process with nucleation; but beyond that, it will not have any noticeable effect on cooking temperature or time.

Salt raises water's boiling point and lowers its freezing point. This means that the water will need to reach a higher temperature before it begins to boil. That is, more salt means more boil time. But, normally, the amount of salt that we usually add to water when cooking is not large enough to make a significant (or even noticeable) difference in the boiling point. From general chemistry, the fact that dissolving a salt in a liquid, such as water, affects its boiling point comes under the general heading of *colligative* properties of materials. As a general phenomenon, if you dissolve one substance (the solute, e.g., salt) in another (the solvent, e.g., water), you will raise the boiling point of the solvent. In fact, any non-volatile soluble substance will raise the boiling point of water. That is why antifreeze (ethylene glycol) provides boiling protection in summer as it simultaneously provides freezing protection in the winter.

Sugar in Water: Why does sugar not increase the boiling point of water as much as salt does? The increase in boiling point depends on the number of molecules you add to the liquid. Salt has a very small molecule. In addition it splits into two particles when in water, the sodium atom and the chloride atom. In numbers: if you add 6g of salt into water, you add about 4,400,000,000,000,000,000,000 ($4.4*10^{22}$) particles to the water. Sugar has a molecular weight that is 3 times larger than that of salt. It does not split up in different particles when in water. So adding 6g of sugar into water, you add around 700,000,000,000,000,000,000 particles ($7.3*10^{21}$) to the water. This is still a huge number, but considerably less than with salt. To get the same effect with sugar that you get with salt, you will have to use about 6 times as much sugar as salt. The same is true in principle with lowering the freezing point of liquids. That is the reason why we use salt in winter on our streets and not sugar - as we would need 6 times as much for the same effect. But it would work with sugar too, if you use enough of it.

Hot water freezes faster than cold water: Normally, yes! Under normal circumstances, cold water freezes faster than hot water. However, a strange phenomenon known as the ***Mpemba*** effect can, under some very specific and obscure conditions, make hot water freeze faster than cold water. One possible explanation is that extremely hot water will lose some of its volume to evaporation, with the result that the smaller quantity of water will freeze faster than a larger quantity. So, technically speaking, this is a fact.

Previously boiled water freezes faster than regular water: Fact. At room temperature, water that was once boiled should freeze faster because the dissolved oxygen has been removed.

Previously boiled water boils faster than regular water: Previously boiled water at room temperature should boil faster than water that has never been boiled. Likewise, previously boiled water freezes faster because of having less dissolved oxygen.

Cold water boils faster than hot water: Myth. Although common sense might suggest that if hot water freezes faster, cold water should boil faster. But that is not the case, scientifically. Hot water from the tap boils faster than cold water, if time saving is the goal. If saving energy is the objective, using hot water for boiling does not actually save much in terms of net energy usage. This is because energy (gas or electricity) is used to heat the water from the tap in the first place, through the hot water heater. On the cautionary side, hot water heaters may even introduce sediments and impurities to the water. For this reason, we are often discouraged from using hot water from the tap for cooking purposes or direct consumption.

Water boils faster at high altitude. Fact. This is due to the effect of lower pressure at high altitude. The higher we go, the lower the pressure. Water expands when it boils. High altitude makes that expansion much more readily possible. This means that large increases in altitude can measurably reduce the boiling temperature. For most substances, the freezing point rises, albeit only very slightly, with increased pressure. Tea connoisseurs often comment that high altitude affects the cooking time of tea as well as its taste. While cooking time can be scientifically verified, the taste assertion must be left to the subjective taste buds of tea aficionados. Water is one of the very rare substances that expand upon freezing. Consequently, the temperature at which ice thaws falls very slightly with increased pressure.

Impact of Humidity on Cooking

Although not often seen as a cooking-related issue, humidity does have an impact on cooking. In addition to temperature and pressure, humidity is perhaps the third-ranking factor in how cooking turns out. Just as temperature determines the burnt or raw outcome of cooked meat, humidity content determines how soggy or dry the outcome is. Cold air contains less moisture (humidity) than warm air. For example, each time you open the freezer, warmer and more humidity-laden air creeps into the freezer due to the process of osmosis. Osmosis is the scientific process through which fluids migrate from a region of higher concentration to a region of lower concentration. In our example, humidity migrates from a higher-humidity ambient room air to the lower-humidity freezer compartment. The newly introduced humid air is cooled off by the freezer, thereby releasing moisture. This cooled air crystallizes and is seen as films of ice on freezer food. When food is stored in a freezer bag, it is protected from this "ice invasion," thus preserving its freshness and freezer life longer. The plastic freezer bag also protects the food from its own natural release (outflow) and intake (inflow) of moisture.

During baking or cooking in a conventional oven, the oven air gets warmed up and rarefied, causing it to be able to absorb more moisture. This dries out the food being cooked. Adding more moisture to the air in the oven can alleviate the drying out problem. We can preheat the oven to the desired cooking temperature and then add a measured amount of water in a crucible to the oven. After the water evaporates through boiling, the food to be cooked can then be placed in the oven. Wrapping food in baking bags helps preserve moisture in the food to minimize unnecessary drying out in the oven. By the way, freezer burn is often the result of excessive drying out of food in the freezer that leaves burn-like scalds on the food.

Impact of Humidity on Personal Comfort

The impact of humidity on personal comfort is much more noticeable and understood than the impact on cooking. For example, let us suppose a central home heating-and-air-conditioning unit operates at 72°F and the temperature is maintained constant through effective thermostat setting. In winter, one may feel too cold while feeling too warm in summer --- both at the same temperature of 72°F. The difference is, of course, due to the impact of relative humidity. When air is dry (less humid), the same temperature feels cooler than it does when the air is moist (more humid). So, in winter, the combination of dry air and 72°F temperature may feel too cold while, in summer, the combination of more humid air 72°F temperature may feel too hot. To remedy this discomfort discrepancy, we use humidifiers in winter and humidifiers in summer.

Kitchen Chemistry

The kitchen is full of chemistry and chemical reactions. In the normal course of things, many of these are rarely recognized as scientific phenomenon by cooks who know intimately how to take advantage of the chemical properties of ingredients. One of the interesting phenomena in the kitchen is the transition of matter from one phase to another, with each phase having a specific role in the kitchen's dance of molecules. Regardless of the type of molecule, matter normally exists as a *solid*, a *liquid*, or a *gas*. Without going scientifically overboard, let us discuss some of the basic aspects of solid-liquid-gas transitions useful for kitchen activities.

Solid-Liquid-Gas Phases

Scientists take delight in studying the different phases of matter, particularly the various temperatures and pressures at which one phase changes into another. Each natural material, even food, for that matter, has three states into which it can transition back and forth. The three states are:

- Solid (e.g., snow, ice)

- Liquid (e.g., rain, lake, stream)

- Gas (e.g., water vapor, fog, cloud, steam)

No kitchen can function without water. But water comes in the three basic forms listed above. The gas state is actually water vapor, which is useful for steaming vegetables and other delicate cooking ingredients. Clouds, snow, and rain are all made of up of some form of water. A cloud is comprised of tiny water droplets and/or ice crystals, a snowflake is an aggregate of many ice crystals, and rain is just liquid water. Water existing as a gas is called water vapor. When referring to the amount of moisture in the air, we are actually referring to the amount of water vapor. If the air is described as "moist," that means the air contains large amounts of water vapor.

Sublimation

In addition to the phase transitions illustrated above, a chemical conversion is also possible through sublimation, which is the process in which a substance is converted directly from a solid to a gas or from a gas to a solid without an intermediate liquid phase.

A solid has a definite shape and volume. A liquid has a definite volume but it takes the shape of a container whereas a gas fills the entire volume of a container. A phase is a distinct and homogeneous state of a system with no visible boundary separating it into parts. Conversion between these states is called a phase transition. Water is the most common substance that its gas (steam), liquid (water), and solid (ice) phases are widely known. An ice water mixture has two phases, so are systems containing ice-and-vapor, and water-and-vapor. To recognize the vapor system in these systems may require a keen observation, because the vapor usually blends with air, and is not detected directly. In a solid the molecules have no motion, and no energy.

The Fourth State of Matter

Plasma is known as the fourth state of matter after the three states of solid, liquid and gas. In most cases, matter on Earth has electrons that orbit around the atom's nucleus. The negatively charged electrons are attracted to the positively charged nucleus. Yes, opposites do attract in the atom world. So, the electrons stay in orbit around the nucleus. When temperatures get extremely hot, the electrons can escape out of their orbit around the atom's nucleus. When the electrons leave the nucleus, they leave behind a positively charged ion. When electrons are no longer trapped in orbits around the nucleus, we have the plasma state. This is when a gas becomes a collection of electrons, which have escaped the pull of the nucleus and ions which are positively charged because they have lost one or more electrons. In the plasma state (aka supercritical state), a substance acts like a gas in some ways and like a liquid in some other ways. Most of the matter in the universe is found in the plasma state. Stars constitute much of the matter in the universe and they are so hot that their matter can only exist in the plasma state. With regard to the above definition of plasma, lightening is best classified as a plasma. We can rest assured that the plasma state does not exist in our kitchens. We certainly hope not.

Food Breadth

Good oral hygiene is an essential part of enjoying your food experiences. Most people associate certain foods with bad breadth. But only in certain cases is this true. Bad breadth is a social embarrassment that happen to anyone because it has diverse causes. In addition to poor oral hygiene, other possible causes of bad breadth include:

- Bacteria on the tongue

- Dry mouth

- Eating foods with strong odor

- Infection

- Smoking

- Alcohol

As an example, the indigenous Nigerian practice of using herbal chewing sticks to clean teeth has been pharmacologically shown to aid good oral hygiene. Dry mouth is particularly a common, but unrecognized, cause of bad breadth that can happen to anyone. A summary of self-care and preventative practices to wade off bad breadth include the following:

- Prevent dry mouth by keeping the mouth hydrated. Drink plenty of water regularly.

- Eat or chew at regular intervals to keep the mouth moist.

- Practice good oral hygiene by brushing teeth and tongue regularly.

- If applicable, clean dentures and ensure they fit properly in the mouth.

- Don't smoke.

- Limit the consumption of alcohol.

- If possible, use baking soda toothpaste

- Don't rely entirely on mouthwash or mints. They work by masking bad breadth and only provide temporary relief. In some cases, they can actually fuel bad breadth by making the mouth dry.

- Chew sugarless gum.

- Suck on lemon drops, which help make saliva and wash away food particles.

- Eat oranges to moisten and freshen the mouth.

Science of Garlic Breadth

Scientifically, after chewing and swallowing garlic, sulfur-containing gases pass through the gut, then circulate throughout the body. The compounds in garlic are morph into nastier forms. With time, the gases are excreted by the lungs. And they increase acetone in the breath, making it outright pungent. So, when "garlic breath" occurs, it is due to exhaling the smelly gases from the lungs, not from the mouth. No amount of brushing, gargling or chewing red-hot chili peppers can stop the exhaled gases.

Chapter 4

KITCHEN PROJECT MANAGEMENT

Pots and pans can get in the way of good organization in the kitchen. So, it is essential to get proactively organized. Project management is a good way to get a kitchen organized and functioning as expected. It is not only about the food coming out of the kitchen. It is also about the process of getting the food prepared. A disorganized kitchen can lead to disastrous outputs from the kitchen. This is an area that is often neglected in food preparation endeavors. Kitchen projects should be managed just like any other project. A clean slate provides a clean output. An organized kitchen provides a well-organized culinary output.

The tools and techniques of project management are directly applicable to large-scale cooking projects. In this case, we are focusing on large-scale cooking for social events rather than institutional undertakings, like restaurants. A project is conventionally defined as "a unique one-of-a-kind endeavor with a definite beginning and a definite end." Large-scale cooking project do, indeed, have all the makings a conventional project and should be managed accordingly. A project is constituted to achieve one or more of the following three outputs:

1. Produce a physical product

2. Provide a certain service

3. Generate a desired result

A cooking project meets all three of the above output categories. Cooking produces a physical consumable product in terms of menu items. Cooking, particularly through a catering business, provides a service in terms helping to meet the needs of the client to provide food for guests and visitors. Cooking, if done properly, will generate the desired result of quenching hunger while satisfying the palate. Project management is an integral part of human existence and a key factor in achieving operational excellence in technical, professional, and domestic functions. For large-scale cooking projects, the proof of project management pudding is in what comes out of the kitchen.

Seventy-nine percent or more of us are homemakers. Homemakers are not necessarily stay-at-home moms. Even where the percentages inferred from research studies don't correlate, we see more and more, working moms and dads also managing home projects. Kitchen-based projects are particularly common. This makes it imperative to apply project management tools and techniques in the kitchen to save time and improve the cooking process. In order to get the best output of your kitchen, you must manage the kitchen enterprise just as you would manage any personal or professional project.

Based on the definition of homemakers utilized by the U.S. Census Bureau, homemakers are individuals who perform duties or "projects" at home that include home-keeping, cooking, making beds, doing laundry, washing dishes, dusting, assembling products, installing gadgets, managing electronics, monitoring utilities, organizing garages, shoveling snow, decorating, and making household repairs. Homemakers also advise families, provide healthcare, and mete out discipline to kids. These are a whole lot of projects (small or big, easy or difficult, simple or complex) *running* around the home. Each and every one of them needs help from project management.

In his professional project management textbook, Deji defines project management as "the process of managing, allocating, and timing resources to accomplish objectives in an efficient and expeditious manner."

Steps of Project Management: The objectives of a project may be stated in terms of time (schedule), performance (quality), or cost (budget). Time is often the most critical aspect of managing any project. Time must be managed concurrently with all other important aspects of any project, particularly in an academic setting. Project management covers the basic stages listed below:

1. Initiation

2. Planning

3. Execution

4. Tracking and Control

5. Closure

The stages are often contracted or expanded based on the needs of the specific project. They can also overlap based on prevailing project scenarios. For example, tracking and control often occur concurrently with project execution. Embedded within execution is the function of activity scheduling. If contracted, the list of stages may include only Planning, Organizing, Scheduling, and Control. In this case, closure is seen as a control action. If expanded, the list may include additional explicit stages such as Conceptualization, Scoping, Resource Allocation, and Reporting. The figures below show the typical steps of project management and a plot of the project lifecycle curve.

Project Initiation

In the first stage of the project lifecycle, the scope of the project is defined along with the approach to be taken to deliver the desired results. The project manager and project team are appointed based on skills, experience, and relevance. The process of organizing the project is often carried out as a bridge or overlap between initiation and planning. The most common tools used in the initiation stage are Project Charter, Business Plan, Project Framework, Overview, Process Mapping, Business Case Justification, and Milestone Reviews. Project initiation normally takes place after problem identification and project definition.

Project Planning

The second stage of the project lifecycle includes a detailed identification and assignment of tasks making up the project. It should also include a risk analysis and a definition of criteria for the successful completion of each deliverable. During planning, the management process is defined, stakeholders are identified, reporting frequency is established, and communication channels are agreed upon. The most common tools used in the planning stage are Brainstorming, Business Plan, Process Mapping, and Milestones Reviews.

Execution and Control

The most important issue in the execution and control stages of the project lifecycle involves ensuring that tasks are executed expeditiously in accordance with the project plan, which is always subject to re-planning. Tracking is an implicit component and prerequisite for project control. For projects that are organized for producing physical products, a design resulting in a specific set of product requirements is created. The integrity of the product is assured through prototypes, validation, verification, and testing. As the execution phase progresses, groups across the organization become progressively involved in the realization of the project objectives. The most common tools or methodologies used in the execution stage include Risk Analysis, Balance Scorecards, Business Plan Review, and Milestone Assessment.

Project Closure

In the closure stage, the project is phased-out or formally terminated. The closure process is often gradual as the project is weaned of resources and personnel are reallocated to other organizational needs. Acceptance of deliverables is an important part of project closure. The closure phase is characterized by a formal project review covering the following components: a formal acceptance of the final product, Weighted Critical Measurements (matching the initial requirements with the final product delivered), thanking and rewarding the participants, documentation of a list of lessons learned, releasing project resources, doing a formal project closure, and project cleanup. Deji does use project management techniques in his kitchen and home projects.

Project Tips for the Kitchen

- Plan your cooking project and execute the project according to plan.

- Have contingency plans in case things don't go well.

- Always allow enough time for your cooking project. Quality takes time. A rushed cooking project could become a failed project.

- Manage your kitchen time judiciously. Distractions cost time. Rework also costs time. Preempt accidents and errors that will cost you time in your cooking project.

- For safety reasons, never leave the handle of a pot on the stove hanging over the edge of the stove. Kitchen accidents, even minor ones, cost time in terms of emergency, personal injury, and recovery time.

- Never leave hot food or appliances unattended while cooking. If you are frying, boiling, or broiling food, stay with your **project** in the kitchen. Project monitoring and oversight are essential for any successful project.

- Avoid engaging in a kitchen project if you are impaired due to the influence of medication or drugs.

- Keep anything that can catch on fire at least three feet from the stove, toaster oven, burners, or other heat sources.

- Keep the stovetop, burners, and oven clean before, during, and after each cooking project.

- Do not wear loose fitting clothes when you are cooking. A fire hazard can detract from project success.

- If all the stove burners are not in use when you cook, use the back row burners. This allows for more operational space around the focal point of your project. This also minimizes the risk of a child reaching for any hot stuff on the cooking surface.

- Keep appliance cords coiled, away from the counter edges, and out of reach of children.

- Use oven mitts or pot-holders when carrying hot food.

- Open hot containers from the microwave slowly and away from your face.

- Never use a wet oven mitt, as it presents a scalding risk if the moisture in the mitt is heated.

- Never hold a child while cooking, carrying or drinking hot foods or liquids. Multi-tasking with kid care is a no-no in the kitchen zone.

The Passion and Dynamics of Nigerian Recipes

The passion for food is most readily demonstrated through the compilation of recipes. Recipes express our gastronomic desires. What is a recipe? A recipe is defined as a formula, method, or process, or procedure for accomplishing a goal. In this case, the goal is a gastronomical output, which is visually appealing and enticing to ingest. Nigerians typically cook from experience rather than from written recipes. This lack of documentation often impedes the adoption of Nigerian foods on the international scene, even though they are widely embraced, accepted, admired, and savored. Nigerian parties are known to be very popular in Europe and North America for the smorgasbord of ethnic Nigerian dishes that they offer. Moin-moin (aka bean cake) is particularly much sought after. Europeans and Americans married to Nigerians often desperately desire recipes of how they can make the delicious Nigerian dishes they have come to love. They often report attempts to recreate what they have sampled either at home or at parties. A common expression of frustration goes something like, "it just doesn't come out the same. It never comes out right for me."

Hopefully, the collection of recipes presented in the following chapters will add to the growing body of publications of recipes to document and perpetrate Nigerian dishes. Part II of this book is one such archival documentation of Nigerian recipes, complemented by a few other ethnic recipes from around the world.

Goat Meat Barbecue

Although pork is the king of barbecue in the American cuisine, some Nigerians don't eat pork either for religious reasons or personal reasons. Meanwhile, goat meat is a favorite for all Nigerians. So, it makes sense to adapt the conventional western barbecue recipes and practices for goat meat. So, here goes:

Ingredients:

¼ cup brown sugar

2 Tbsp chili powder

1 Tbsp salt

1 tsp black pepper

1 tsp dried oregano

½ tsp cayenne

½ tsp garlic powder

½ tsp onion powder

Goat ribs (sized to 2 racks of beef baby back ribs)

1 cup low-sodium chicken broth (liquid ingredient)

2 Tbsp apple cider vinegar (liquid ingredient)

Barbecue sauce (liquid ingredient)

Instructions:

In a small bowl, combine the dry ingredients

Pat the ribs dry with paper towels

Rub the ingredients mixture onto both sides of ribs

Refrigerate 1 hour, up to overnight

Preheat oven to 250^{0}F

In a roasting pan, combine 1 cup low-sodium chicken broth and 2 Tbsp apple cider vinegar

Add ribs to the liquid mixture

Cover pan tightly with foil

Bake 2 ½ hours

Transfer ribs from pan to a platter

Pour liquid from pan into a saucepan

Bring to a boil

Reduce heat

Simmer 5 minutes or until reduced by half

In a large bowl, combine the reduced liquid and 1 cup barbecue sauce

Grill ribs 5 minutes on each side or until browned and slightly charred

Add ribs to bowl with barbecue sauce mixture

Toss around to coat as evenly as possible

Enjoy!

Note: The same grilling process can be adapted for roasting cow leg as a part of culinary creativity.

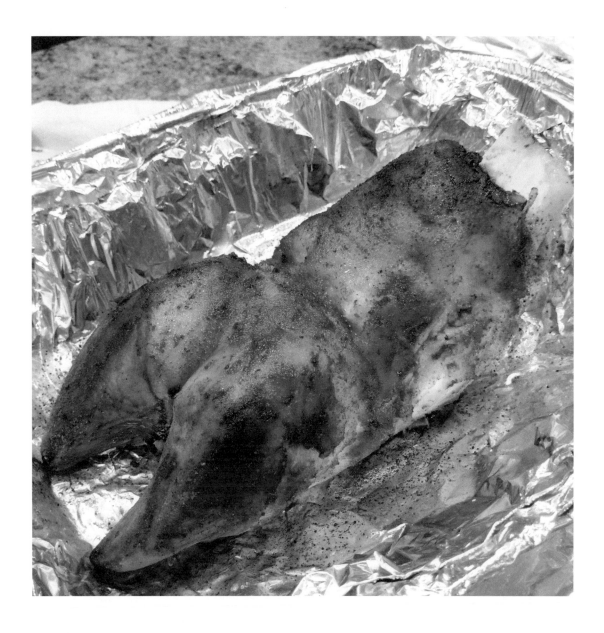

Berried Rice

Suitable for main dish any time of day

Ingredients:

Long-grain rice

Dried red berries

Directions:

1. Cook long-grain rice as usual

2. Just before final stage, sprinkle dried red berries on the rice

3. Berried Rice (original recipe with red berries buried within the grains of rice)

4. Enjoy as usual as steamed white rice

Fried Crab Eggs

Suitable for general snack

Ingredients:

10 to 15 female blue crabs. Females laden with eggs are usually available in Asian grocery stores at various times of the year.

Directions:

1. Clean crabs in cold water

2. Steam cleaned crabs in a large pot

3. When cooked, the color will change to reddish-orange color

4. Crab open the belly of each crab and extract the reddish-orange clumps of egg

5. Fry the extracted egg slightly in olive oil or vegetable oil

6. Enjoy as a snack on sliced bread or alone

Ogi/Akamu/Koko/ (Corn Custard)

Mostly for breakfast

Serves 2 - 3

Ingredients:

1 cup corn powder

4 cups boiling water

1 cup cold water

Milk or evaporated milk – to taste

Sugar – to taste

Directions:

Two methods to prepare this breakfast:

Method One:

- In a bowl, combine corn powder, sugar, and 1 ½ cup of cold water; mix till the texture is smooth and lump free.

- Pour 3 cups of the boiling water over the mixture (the mixture will rise up as you pour the boiling water); cover for two minutes. For thinner ogi use more boiling water.

- Open and stir the Ogi; add more sugar as needed to taste.

- Pour about half (1/2) cup of warm milk or warm water over the Ogi or to taste and serve.

Method Two:

- In a deep pot, combine corn powder, sugar, and five (5) cups of cold water; mix till the texture is smooth and lump free.

- Cook mixture at medium high on the stove; continuously stirring till mixture thickens to avoid lump; reduce heat to avoid splashing and cook for five (5) minutes. Add more water for thinner Ogi.

- Pour into a bowl; pour warm milk or warm water over the Ogi; more sugar and milk to taste as needed.

- Serve with Akara or Moin-moin.

Note: For thicker Ogi use less water and for richer Ogi use milk instead of water.

Éko (Corn Powder Jell) make with Ogi (Corn Powder)

Suitable for snack or accompaniment for main dish

Ingredients:

2 cup Ogi (Corn Powder)

10 -10 ½ cups cold water

Directions:

- Mix corn powder with five (5) cups of cold water in a deep cooking pot till smooth and lump free then add five (5) more cups of water and stir.

- Cook mixture at medium high heat and stir continuously with a wooden spatula to avoid lumps forming and to avoid splashing; as you continue stirring, mixture will begin to thicken slowly; continue stirring till it thicken and lump free.

- If lumps are forming, it means the heat is too high, so reduce the heat.

- When the mixture has completely thickened like Custard, reduce heat to low; add half (½) cup of water and cover; cook for 3-5 minutes. Open and stir thoroughly.

- To check if Eko is done, drop a small amount into some cold water in a bowl, if it sets and floats then it is done.

- Dish Eko into small individual bowls and let cool down completely at room temperature or make pouches/pockets with Aluminum Foil, then fill the pouches about 2/3 full; seal the foil at the top by folding several times; cool at room temperature completely.

- Open and Enjoy!

Serve with <u>Akara</u>, Moin-Moin, soup or pepper soup.

Akara (Beans Patties)

Suitable for snack or meal accompaniment

Ingredients:

1 lb. Bag Blackeye Peas or African Red Beans

1 small red bell pepper

1 small to medium onion

2 maggi or knorr cubes – crushed

2 cups water

Oil or African palm oil – to fry

Salt to taste

Instructions:

Cleaning and Instructions: of the beans

- Soak blackeye peas in cold water for about five minutes. (This will allow the beans to swell up and make it easy to remove the outer coat); or pour small amount of the beans into the blender, cover with water; grind for about 3 – 5 seconds (do not blend) and pour the beans into a large bowl; continue the process till finish.

- Cover beans with water; rub beans in between palms of both hands back and forth in the water to loosen the outer coat. The outer coat will naturally float to the top.

- Use a strainer to separate beans from the outer coat by draining the floating coats. Continue this process till beans is cleaned and no more coats or dark sport. Filter and change water as many times as needed.

Blending

- Combine cleaned beans, bell pepper, onion and blend. Add water as needed for the blender to rotate; however, do not add too much water or it will become watery). **The beans batter (paste) should look like Pancake batter.**

- Pour blended beans into a mixing bowl; add crushed maggi cubes and salt if needed. Mix thoroughly till lump free and light.

Frying

- Deep-fry the mixture by scooping a little amount individually into hot oil and fry till golden. Scoop as many as the frying pan will take.

- Continue the process till finish.

Serve with Ogi, Eko, custard, Quaker Oat, pap or bread. Also serve as appetizer or snack.

Moin-Moin (Steamed Beans Cake)

Instructions:

1 lb. bag Blackeye Peas or African Red Beans

1 medium red bell pepper

1 medium onion

2 pieces dry fish (shredded) or 1 can corned beef

2 crayfish maggi cubes – crushed

3 – 4 cups water

¼ cup palm oil or oil - warm

Salt to taste

Instructions:

Cleaning of the Beans

Step 1

- Soak blackeye peas in cold water for about five minutes. (This will allow the beans to swell up and make it easy to remove the outer coat); or pour small amount of the beans into the blender, cover with water; grind for about 3 – 5 seconds (do not blend) and pour the beans into a large bowl; continue the process till finish.

- Cover beans with water; rub beans in between palms of both hands back and forth in the water to loosen the outer coat. The outer coat will naturally float to the top.

- Use a strainer to separate beans from the outer coat by draining the floating coats. Continue this process till beans is cleaned and no more coats or dark sport. Filter and change water as many times as needed.

Blending

- Combine cleaned beans, bell pepper, and onion and blend till mixture becomes a smooth paste. (Add water as needed for the blender to rotate. However, do not add too much or it will become watery). **The beans batter (paste) should be a little thinner than Pancake batter.**

Step 2

- Make pouches/pockets with aluminum foil or use individual non-stick cup cake cups.

- Shred dry fish and clean in hot water.

- Warm palm oil or oil.

- Pour blended beans into a mixing bowl; add shredded fish or corned beef, crushed maggi and mix; add warm palm oil; salt if needed and mix thoroughly until lump free.

- The beans batter should be a little bite thinner than cake batter (not too thick or too thin).

- Scoop the blended beans into the aluminum pouches one by one; fill half-way to allow room for expansion during cooking. Seal the foil at the top by folding several times.

- Arrange moin-moin into a deep cooking pot and add about 3 - 4 cups of water. Add more if needed.

- Cook for 30 - 45 minutes at medium high.

- Open one to check if it is done. Moin-moin is done when it is firm to the touch after exposure to the air for few minutes.

- Unwrap, slice and serve.

Serving Suggestion: serve with Ogi, Eko, Rice, and with drinking (soak) Gari, Custard, Quaker Oat or as snack.

Fried Egg (Nigerian Style)

Ingredients:

4 Eggs

1 small onion – diced

1 small red pepper – diced

1 medium fresh tomato – diced

Some hot red pepper – optional

Oil – any type

2 knorr or maggi cubes

Salt to taste

Instructions:

On a medium heat sauté onion, red pepper, hot pepper.

Add 1 or 2 maggi cubes; mix and remove from stove.

Beat the eggs together, add pepper mixture and mix.

Fry on both sides to your like.

Note: You can mix corned beef or sardine with eggs and fry.

Serve with bread, boiled yam and boiled potatoes.

To further garnish the fried egg, you may prepare parboiled eggs, cut the eggs in half, and use the halved eggs to decorate around the edge of the plated fried eggs.

Scotch Eggs

Ingredients:

1 dozen eggs

2-3 lbs. Turkey, chicken, or regular sausage

Breadcrumbs to coat - Finely crushed and seasoned

Flour to coat – Seasoned

2 knorr or maggi cubes - crushed

Ground red pepper to taste - optional

Salt to taste

Oil for frying

Inst ructions:

- Boil 6 eggs. Set aside to cool down completely and peel.

- If frozen sausage is used, thaw completely at room temperature.

- Combine the sausage meat with crushed maggi or knorr cubes and mix thoroughly in a bowl.

- Mold sausage meat mixture around the outer layer of each cooked egg one by one.

- In a separate bowl, mix three (3) eggs. Use more eggs if needed.

- In separate bowls, mix breadcrumbs and flour with some pepper and salt for seasoning.

- Dip each molded egg in the beaten eggs; then roll in the breadcrumbs; then in the flour, if necessary dip back in the mix egg and then in the breadcrumbs once more.

- Deep fry eggs in hot oil until golden and crisp and the sausage meat is completely cooked.

- Carefully remove scotch eggs from the hot oil and drain.

- Use very little flour to rub both hands if sticking.

- Be careful with hot oil. Do not leave unattended.

Serve whole or slice each one in half for appetizer or as snack.

Boiled African Yam served with fried Eggs

Ingredients:

1 large African yam

2-3 cups of water (more if needed)

2-3 tablespoon sugar (adjust to taste) - optional

Salt to taste

6 - 8 eggs

Directions:

- Peel the skin off the yam, slice, and wash in cold water.

- Arrange sliced Yam into a cooking pot; add water, sugar and salt.

- Cook until yam is tender (cooked) (20 -25 minutes).

- Remove from heat, drain any leftover water; set aside.

- Fry the eggs any way and serve over yam.

Serve with fried eggs, stew, enjoy plan with butter, margarine or palm oil.

Fried African Yam

Ingredients:

1 large African yam

Salt to taste

Hot red ground pepper – optional

Vegetable Oil

Instructions:

- Peel the skin off the yam; slice or dice; and wash in cold water.

- Drain and dry the slices of yam with paper towel or air dry.

- Sprinkle with salt and pepper to taste.

- Deep fry in any oil or palm oil till golden brown.

Serve with fried stew, fried eggs or enjoy plain with butter or margarine.

Fried Plantain and Fried Eggs

Ingredients:

6 pieces of ripped plantain

Salt to taste

Oil (any type) or palm oil

6-8 eggs

Instructions:

- Slice or dice the plantain into pieces; add salt to taste.

- Pour oil or palm oil into a deep fryer or frying pan over medium high heat until hot.

- Place some cut plantain into the hot oil and fry until golden brown.

- Remove from the oil or palm oil and continue the process till finish.

- Fry eggs; place dodo on a flat plate and top with fried eggs

- Serve hot.

Buns (Nigerian Donuts)

Ingredients:

½ bag 5 lbs. All-purpose flour

1 ½ - 2 cups of sugar or adjust to taste

6 large eggs

1 cup butter

½ teaspoon salt

9 - 10 tablespoon water

Instructions:

- In a large mixing bowl add flour and knead in butter; add sugar and salt.

- Add eggs and knead; add water little by little and knead into dropping consistency.

- Pour oil into a deep fryer; let it gets hot (test the oil by dropping a little batter into the hot oil); batter will float to the top if oil is hot enough.

- Roll batter into individual balls (determine the size) and gently drop into the hot oil or batter can be scooped up by forming a scoop with your hand and scoop up the batter and gently drop into the hot oil. Please be careful with this method.

- Deep fry until light brown or golden brown. Make sure buns are fried through to the inner part. Remove and drain excess oil.

- Serve hot. Okay to warm in the microwave oven.

Puff-Puff (Nigerian Donut)

Ingredients:

½ bag lbs. All-purpose flour

2 cups of sugar or adjust to taste

2 sachets quick-rising yeast

1 tsp. salt

7-8 cups of very warm water

Instructions:

- In a large bowl, combine flour, sugar, yeast, salt and mix.

- Pour very warm water slowly and mix till desire softness or thickness and lumps free with hand.

- Cover mixed batter and set aside to rise for about three to four hours in a warm or hot spot in the house or outside in the sun. Batter can be mixed and set aside to rise over night also.

Frying:

- Pour oil into a deep fryer; let it gets hot; (test the oil by dropping a little batter into the hot oil); batter will float to the top if oil is hot enough.

- Use a scooper, 1/8 of a cup size, or 1/4 of a cup size to scoop up the batter and gently drop into the hot oil to form a ball.

- Also batter can be scooped up by forming a scoop with your hand and scoop up the batter and gently drop into the hot oil. Please be careful with this method.

- Deep fry until light brown or golden brown.

- Continue this process till the batter is finished.

- Optional: Sprinkle puff-puff with powdered sugar.

Serve hot. Okay to warm in the microwave oven.

Meat Pie

Meat pies are popular for snacks. In our personal recollection, the best commercial meat pies we know of were those that Kingsway Store on Broad Street in Lagos, Nigeria used to make in the 1960s and 1970s. Such high-quality meat pies are hard to come by these days.

Ingredients:

Meat Mixture:

1 ib. ground beef or turkey

1 ib. ground turkey sausage

2 medium peel potatoes – diced

1 10¾ oz. can Cream of Mushroom Condensed Soup

1 medium onion – chopped

1 medium red bell pepper - chopped

1 medium green bell pepper – chopped

2 pieces of habaneras or hot chili pepper

4 cloves garlic - chopped

2 Tablespoon Chopped Ginger

½ teaspoon curry powder

½ cup Milk

2 knorr or maggi cubes

Salt to taste

When making meat pies, it is best to start with the pastry dough first. The Dough needs to rest for about 3-4 hours before use; unless refrigerated pie crusts are used.

Meat mixture instructions

- Sauté diced potatoes for about 5 minutes; then add chopped onion, bell peppers, habaneras or hot chili pepper, garlic, ginger, curry powder and maggi or knorr cubes. Add ¼ cup of water if needed and sauté; set aside.

- Brown ground beef and turkey sausage in a skillet; stirring to crumble the meat (drain any excess fat). Add pepper mixture and mix thoroughly. Set aside to cool. This gives the meat mixture to soak up any juice.

Dough mixture

5 cups All-purpose flour

2 ½ cups unsalted butter or margarine – cubed and keep cold

4 egg yolks

8 tablespoon cold water

3 tablespoon sugar - optional

Egg white for brushing

Instructions:

- Combine flour and butter in a mixing bowl and knead; then add egg yolks, sugar, and knead the dough.

- Then, add the cold water gradually little by little into the dough to form soft but firm dough.

- Roll dough into a ball and wrap with a clear plastic wrap; let it rest for about four (4) hours in the fridge.

- The number of pies from the dough will depend on the size of the pies.

- Roll out some dough, about 1/4 inch in thickness (don't make it too thick);

- Take a round object, place it on the dough and cut a circle out; then add one tablespoon of the meat mixture in the center of the dough.

- Then fold the dough over the meat mixture and pinch the edges together using a fork so the filling is sealed. Repeat the above steps till out of dough or meat mixture.

- In a separate bowl, mix the egg white and brush the exterior of the meat pies before baking.

- Arrange meat pies on a baking tray (spray or grease the tray).

- Bake at 350 for 25 minutes or until brown or golden brown.

Serve with Orange juice, Milk, Tea or coffee.

Sausage Rolls

Ingredients:

1 ib. Turkey sausage or sausage of choice

1 small onion – finely chopped

1 large carrot – peeled and grated

Some ginger to taste

Some garlic to taste

2 medium eggs

Some milk to brush the sausage roll

½ tsp. ground black pepper

1-2 maggi or knorr cubes

Instructions:

- Combine sausage, onion, carrot, ginger, garlic, black pepper, maggi cubes and eggs in a large bowl and mix thoroughly.

- Divide sausage mixture into four (4) and roll out to about four (4) inches long each.

- To make dough see (Meat Pie) or use readymade dough from store.

- Place rolled sausage on one end edge of dough and roll up to enclose mixture; then cut into 2 pieces each.

- Arrange sausage rolls on a tray (oil the tray first); place seam side down.

- Brush sausage rolls top with milk.

- Bake for 20 – 25 minutes or until golden brown.

- Cool and serve.

Serve with Orange juice, Milk, Tea or coffee.

Eba (Gari) – Cassava Grits

Serve with stew of meat or fish

Ingredients:

4 cups of water

2 cups of Gari

Instructions:

- Boil water in a deep pot.

- Remove one cup of the boiling water and set aside for later use.

- Reduce the heat to medium heat to avoid splashing.

- Using a wooden spoon, stir Gari slowly into the water.

- Stir to break up lumps until a smooth consistency is obtained.

- Add remaining hot water **only if needed** to get softer Eba or to your like then dish out.

- Because Gari is a little coarse, the resulting Eba will be a little coarse. Sift Gari to make the Eba less coarse.

Serve Eba with any vegetable soup, okra soup, egusi soup, or ewedu and stew.

Amala

Yam Flour Mix - Serve with any soup in this book

Ingredients:

5 cups of water

2 cups of Amala flour

Instructions:

- Boil water in a deep pot.

- Remove one (1) cup of the boiling water and set aside for later use.

- Reduce the heat to medium heat to avoid splashing.

- Using a wooden spoon, pour Elubo into the water and mix continuously to break up lumps until a smooth consistency is obtained.

- Add remaining hot water as needed slowly for softer Amala.

- Cover the pot and cook slowly for five (5) minutes, then mix thoroughly and dish out.

Serve Amala hot and eaten with any vegetable soup, okra soup, egusi soup, or ewedu and stew. Amala is a favorite substitute for pounded yam and eba in the Abeokuta region of Nigeria.

Pounded Yam (Iyan) Using Yam Flour

Pounded Yam (Using Yam Flour) - Serve with any soup in this book

Ingredients:

5 cups of water

2 cups of Iyan flour

Instructions:

- Boil water in a deep pot.

- Remove one (1) cup of the boiling water and set aside for later use.

- Reduce the heat to medium heat to avoid splashing.

- Using a wooden spoon, stir Iyan slowly into the water and continue mixing.

- Mix thoroughly to break up lumps until a smooth consistency is obtained.

- Add remaining hot water slowly as needed for softer pounded yam.

- Cook Iyan slowly for five (5) minutes more, then mix thoroughly and dish out.

Serve Iyan with any vegetable soups, okra soup, egusi soup, or ewedu and stew.

Pounded Yam (Iyan) Using Fresh Yam

Ingredients:

1 large Fresh Yam

Water

Mortar and Pestle or any substitute

Instructions:

- Peel the skin off the yam and rinse in cold water.

- Slice or cut the yam into pieces.

- Arrange sliced yam into a deep cooking pot and add water to cover the yam.

- Cook yam until very soft.

- Remove yam from heat; drain left over water and set aside.

- Place small amount of yam in the mortar and pound with the pestle, add more yam and pound; continue till no more yam left.

- Continue pounding till you get firm softer dough with the same consistency.

- Add the set aside water or warm water as needed for softer Iyan or to your like.

Serve Iyan with any vegetable soups, okra soup, egusi soup, Agbono, or awedu and stew.

Semolina Fufu

Serve with beef or fish stew or soup (similar to fufu, eba, amala, etc.)

Ingredients:

5 cups of water

2 cups of Semolina

Instructions:

- Boil water in a deep pot.

- Remove one cup of the boiling water and set aside for later use.

- Reduce the heat to medium heat to avoid splashing.

- Using a wooden spoon, stir Semolina slowly into the water and mix.

- Mix well to break up lumps until a smooth consistency is obtained.

- Add remaining hot water slowly as needed to get the right consistency and softer Semolina.

- Mix thoroughly then dish out.

Serve Semolina with any vegetable soups, okra soup, egusi soup, ogbono, or ewedu and stew.

Pepper Stew

This Nigerian stew is a special blend of tomatoes (fresh or canned), onion, fresh hot red pepper, ginger, garlic, favorite seasoning, and vegetable oil or palm oil.

Ingredients:

2 lbs. assorted meat – cube (See list of assorted meat below)

2 15¼ oz. can tomato sauce

1 6oz. can tomato paste

1 large onion

Fresh Ginger – to your taste

Fresh Garlic – to your taste

3 habanera peppers (hot, adjust to taste)

2 red bell peppers

4 maggi or knorr cubes

½ cup oil – less if prefer

Water

Salt to taste

Instructions:

- Blend tomato sauce, paste, onion, ginger, garlic, habanera peppers and red bell peppers together; add water as needed for the blender to rotate and blend until smooth). Set aside.

- In a deep cooking pot, boil assorted meat with any meat seasoning until tender. Meat and honeycomb (tripe) will become tender before cow skin; so, remove these and continue cooking cow skin until tender or boil the cow skin separately.

- Add meat and honeycomb back to the cow skin after it is done. (Note: add very little water as most meats already have built-in liquid). Set aside.

- In a deep cooking pot, combine blended tomato/pepper mixture; maggi or knorr and cook for 20 minutes. Stir occasionally during cooking to avoid burning the sauce. Add ½ to one cup of water if mixture appears thick or as needed and cook for five minutes.

- Add assorted meats; mix and cook for 15 minutes.

- Add oil, cover and cook at low to medium heat for 15 – 20 minutes. Stir occasionally during cooking to prevent burning and to allow ingredients to mix evenly.

- Add salt to taste as needed.

Serve over rice or eba, fufu, etc.

Note: If cooking fish, do not boil the fish; clean and cut into pieces, sprinkle with a little salt and set aside for 30 minutes to marinate before cooking. Instead of stirring soup, lift the pot and shake to mix the ingredients.

Meat options: Goat meat, beef chunks, chicken, guinea fowl, turkey, oxtail, beef tripe, cow skin, cow legs, beef tripe, snail, stockfish, etc.

Fish options: Catfish, tilapia, cod, whiting, red snapper, flounder, etc. Catfish and tilapia are the most common fish used in Nigerian soups.

Fried Pepper Stew

With or without meat

Ingredients:

2 15¼oz. can tomato sauce	2 red bell peppers
1 6oz. can tomato paste	4 maggi or knorr cubes
1 large onion	¼ teaspoon curry powder
Fresh Ginger – to your taste	¼ teaspoon ground thyme
Fresh Garlic – to your taste	2-3 cups of Oil or more
3 habanera peppers (hot, adjust to taste)	Salt to taste

Instructions:

If adding fish to the stew:

- Dice and clean fresh fish; season with salt and set aside in a strainer for about 20-30 minutes for the water to drain and marinate then fry and Set aside.

If adding meat to the stew:

- Cut into pieces boil with any meat seasoning until tender. (Note: add little water as most meat produces water as it cooks). Remove from the pot and put in a strainer to drain any juice from the meat then fry and set aside.

- Blend tomato sauce, paste, onion, ginger, garlic, habanera peppers, and red bell peppers together; add very little water during blending but enough for the blade to rotate.

- In a deep cooking pot, add mixture of blended tomato/pepper, maggi or knorr, thyme and curry.

- Cover and cook for 30 - 45 minutes or until fairly reduced to thick paste; stir occasionally during cooking to prevent burning; reduce heat if necessary.

- Add fresh oil or use leftover oil from frying the meat or fish; mix and cook for another 10 minutes (the oil will float to the top). However, if oil is not floating on top, continue cooking at a low heat on cover so that the sauce will become condense lowly and the oil will float to the top. Fried stew takes a lot of oil! So add more if needed.

- Add fried meat, snail or fried fish and mix. At a low heat, simmer for another 10 - 15 minutes.

- Add salt if needed to taste.

Serve over rice, beans or any of the soups in this book.

Ewedu (Jute Leaf) Soup

Ewedu soup is enjoyed by the Yoruba people in the Western part of Nigeria.

Ingredients:

2 cups Fresh Ewedu leaves or one bag frozen - chopped

1½ - 2 cups of water

½ tablespoon ground crayfish

1 piece dried fish – shredded

2 tablespoon Egusi (melon) - optional

1 tablespoon Locust beans - optional

1 – 2 maggi or knorr cubes

Salt to taste

Instructions:

- Remove ewedu leaves from the stem; wash very well in cold water to remove grits; drain and air dry.

- Finely chop up ewedu or grate with little water in a blender (do not blend) and set aside.

- Shred and clean dried fish in hot water; set aside.

- Add two cups of water into a small cooking pot; add dried fish, maggi and cook for five (5) minutes; then add Egusi (melon) and cook for 10 minutes.

- Reduce heat and add Ewedu and mix; add ground crayfish, locust beans, and cook for 5-10 minutes.

- Add salt and more water if needed for thinner ewedu.

- Cook for 2-3 minutes.

Serve with Pepper Stew and eat with Amala, Eba, Fufu, Semolina, or Pounded Yam.

Okra Soup

Ingredients:

1 16oz. bag frozen Okra – chopped

2 - 3 cups of water

1 dried fish – shredded (optional)

1 tablespoon ground crayfish (optional)

1- 2 maggi or knorr cubes

Salt to taste

Instructions:

- Finely chop up Okra and set aside.

- In a cooking pot, add two (2) cups of water, maggi or knorr cubes, dried fish and cook for ten (10) minutes.

- Add chopped okra, ground crayfish, stir and cook for five (5) minutes.

- Add more water if Okra appears thick and cook for five (5) minutes more; add salt if needed.

Serve with pepper stew and eat with Amala, Eba, Fufu, Semolina, or Pounded Yam.

Okra Soup with Meat

Ingredients:

1 16oz. bag frozen Okra

1 small size stockfish - chopped

1lb. assorted meats

1 tablespoon ground crayfish

½ tablespoon ground hot red pepper

1 tablespoon bitter leaf

½ cup palm oil or 1/3 cup of oil – increase amount to taste

4 maggi or knorr cubes

Water

Salt to taste

Instructions:

Step 1.

- Chop up Okra (not blend) and set aside.

- In a deep cooking pot, cover stockfish with water and boil with some salt until tender; set aside.

- In a deep cooking pot, boil assorted meat with any meat seasoning until tender. Meat and honeycomb (tripe) will become tender before cow skin; so, remove these and continue cooking cow skin until tender or cook cow skin separately.

- Add meat and honeycomb back to cow skin after it is done. (Note: add very little water because most meats have built-in liquid). Reduce heat to medium and add stockfish to the meat mixture and cook together for a few minutes.

Step 2.

- If there is enough stock in the meat mixture or add 2 – 3 cups of water if needed, add ground red pepper, maggi or knorr cubes and cook for 10 minutes at medium high heat.

- Add bitter leaf, ground crayfish, mix thoroughly and cook for five (5) minutes; add palm oil and cook for another 10 minutes. Mix occasionally to prevent burning.

- Add chopped Okra and cook for another ten (10) minutes uncovered.

- Add more water if soup appears thick little by little; cook for another 2-3 minutes. Mix occasionally during cooking to prevent burning and to allow ingredients to mix evenly.

Serve with Amala, Iyan, Eba, Semolina or Fufu.

Note: There are different variations of this soup depending on the type of assorted meats and fish options.

Assorted Meats: Goat meat, beef, chicken, turkey, beef oxtail, beef tripe, cow skin, cow legs, beef tripe, snail, and stockfish, etc.

Bitter Leaf Soup

Bitter leaf soup is a soup prepared with freshly-washed Bitter Leaves. This soup is popularly eaten by the Igbos from Eastern part of Nigeria.

Ingredients:

12 oz. bag bitter leaf

1 ½ lbs. assorted meat - cubed

1 small stockfish – chopped

2 pieces dried fish – shredded

2 tablespoon ground crayfish

1 small onion - chopped

½ tablespoon ground hot red pepper (adjust to taste)

½ - 1cup palm oil

4 maggi or knorr cubes

Water

Salt to taste

Instructions:

Step 1.

- Wash bitter leaves very well to remove most of the bitterness; soak for about 20 minutes in salted water; drain and set aside.

- Shred dried fish into small pieces and clean in hot water. Set aside.

- In a deep pot, cover stockfish with water and boil with some salt until tender; set aside.

- Boil assorted meat with meat seasoning until tender. (Add water if needed). Meat and honeycomb (tripe) will become tender before cow skin; so, remove these and continue cooking cow skin until tender or boil the cow skin separately.

- Add meat, and honeycomb back into the cow skin after it is done; add stockfish, dried fish, pepper, onion, maggi or knorr, mix and simmer for ten (10) minutes. Keep stock (broth) in it and reduce heat to low to get bitter leaves ready.

Step 2.

- Add clean bitter leaves into the meat mixture and cook for ten (10) minutes.

- Add ground crayfish, palm oil to meat mixture and cook for another 15 minutes at medium heat. Occasionally, stir soup to prevent burning and also to allow ingredients to mix evenly.

- If soup appears thick, add water little by little until desired thickness reached; and salt as needed to taste. Then cook for 5 minutes.

- If soup is watery, use thickener like cooked cocoyam paste.

Serve soup with Eba, Amala, Iyan, Semolina, or Fufu.

There are different variations of this soup; especially the type of meats, or seafood selection.

Some people add cocoyam as a source of thickener for the soup.

Assorted Meats: Goat meat, beef, chicken, turkey, beef oxtail, beef tripe, cow skin, cow legs, beef tripe, snail, stockfish, etc.

Ogbono Soup (aka Apon Soup)

Just like Egusi soup, Apon or Ogbono soup is enjoyed by all Nigerians.

There are different variations of cooking this popular soup.

Ingredients:

¼ cup ground Apon/ Ogbono

2-3 pieces of stockfish – cook and shredded

Some pieces of assorted meat – diced (see list for assorted below)

1 tablespoon ground crayfish (optional)

½ tablespoon ground hot red pepper – or to taste

¼ cup of palm oil or some oil

2 maggi or knorr cubes

Water

Salt to taste

Instructions:

Step 1.

- In a deep pot, cover stockfish with water and boil with some salt until tender; shred and set aside.

- Boil assorted meat with any meat seasoning until tender. Meat and honeycomb (tripe) will become tender before cow skin; so, remove these and continue cooking the cow skin until tender or cook the cow skin separately.

- Add meat and honeycomb back to the cow skin after it is done. (Note: add very little water as most meats contain in-built liquids). Reduce heat to medium and add stockfish, cook for view minutes together. Add pepper, ground crayfish, maggi or knorr cubes, and water if needed; cook for 10 minutes and reduce heat to low to get the Ogbono to reddish color.

Step 2.

- In another pot, add one-and-half (1½) cups of water and bring to boil.

- Reduce heat to medium; stir in Apon/Ogbono slowly and whisk constantly. Ogbono will rise up and draw as you stir; reduce heat if necessary.

- Gradually stir in one (1) cups of water and continuously stirring until a smooth consistency is obtained and lump free. Cook for about 10 - 15 minutes at medium heat.

- Add meat/stockfish mixture into Ogbono; add palm oil; cover and cook for another ten minutes. Stir occasionally during cooking to prevent burning and also to allow ingredients to mix evenly.

- Add more water if soup appears too thick little by little or to your like and simmer for another 10 minutes.

Serve soup with Eba, Amala, Iyan, Semolina, or Fufu.

Ogbono Soup with Okra – Add two (2) cups of chopped Okra (not blend) and some water to the soup at the end; cook for another 5 minutes.

Assorted Meats: Goat meat, beef, chicken, smoked turkey, oxtail, beef tripe, cow skin, cow legs, beef tripe, snail, or stockfish.

Chicken Feet Soup

Prepare using similar ingredients and instructions for other soups provided in this book.

Egusi (Melon) Soup

Egusi soup is a popular Nigerian soup. Cooking techniques differ from region to region. Egusi soup can be prepared with or without meat of fish. Dried fish and dried meats are commonly used.

Ingredients:

1 cup ground Egusi	1 red bell pepper
1 small size stockfish - chopped	2 habanera peppers (hot, adjust to taste)
1 to 1½ ibs assorted meat	Ginger to taste
2 pieces smoked or dried fish (optional) - shredded	4 maggi or knorr cubes
2 Tbsp. ground crayfish	½ cup palm oil or 1/3 cup oil
1 15¼oz. can tomato sauce	Water
2 - 3 tablespoon tomato paste	Salt to taste
1 medium onion	

Instructions:

Step 1.

- In a deep pot, cover stockfish with water and boil with some salt until tender; set aside.

- Shred dried fish into small pieces and clean in hot water. Soak in salted water for about 10 minutes and set aside.

- Blend tomato sauce, paste, onion, habaneras peppers ginger, and red bell peppers; add water as needed for the blender to rotate and blend until smooth).

- In a large pot, boil assorted meat with any meat seasoning until tender. Meat and honeycomb (tripe) will become tender before cow skin; so, remove these and continue cooking cow skin until tender or boil the cow skin separately.

- Add meat and honeycomb back to the cow skin after it is done. (Note: add very little water because most meats have in-built liquids). Reduce heat to medium; add stockfish, smoked fish and simmer together for view minutes.

- Add tomato/pepper mixture, maggi or knorr cubes; mix and cook for 15 - 20 minutes.

- Add 2 cups of water if soup appears too thick or as needed little by little. Stir occasionally during cooking to avoid burning and to mix ingredients evenly.

- Reduce heat to medium heat; add some broth from the soup into Egusi and mix in. Roll Egusi into tiny little balls and drop or sprinkle each one into the meat mixture; cover and cook for fifteen (15) minutes at medium heat; then open and mix.

- Add crayfish and palm oil; cover and cook for 10 minutes; open and mix; then simmer for ten (10) minutes at low heat.

- Add salt and water as needed and cook for 5 minutes at low heat.

Serve this soup with Eba, Amala, Iyan, Semolina or Fufu.

Assorted Meats: Goat meat, beef, chicken, smoked turkey, oxtail, beef tripe, cow skin, cow legs, beef tripe, snail, or stockfish.

Egusi (Melon) and Vegetable Soup

This recipe is an amalgamation of melon soup and vegetable soup.

Ingredients:

1 ½ cup ground Egusi	Fresh Ginger – to your taste
2 16 oz bag Vegetable	Fresh Garlic – to your taste
1 small size stockfish – chopped	3 habanera peppers (hot; adjust to taste)
1½ lbs. assorted meat – cut or diced (see list below)	1 red bell pepper
1 tablespoon ground crayfish	4 maggi or knorr cubes
1 15¼ oz. can tomato sauce	½ -1 cup palm oil or 1/3 cup of oil
2 tablespoon tomato paste	Water
1 medium onion	Salt to taste

Instructions:

Step 1.:

- Soak vegetable in salted water for 20 minutes; drain and remove excess water; set aside.

- In a deep pot, cover stockfish with water and boil with some salt until tender; set aside.

- Shred dried fish into small pieces and clean in hot water; then soak in salted water for about 10 minutes. Set aside.

- Blend tomato sauce, paste, onion, ginger, garlic, habanera peppers, and red bell peppers; add little water during blending but enough for the blade to rotate. Set aside.

Step 2.:

- In a separate bowl, boil assorted meat with any meat seasoning until tender. Meat and honeycomb (tripe) will become tender before cow skin; so, remove these and continue cooking cow skin until tender or cook the cow skin separately.

- Add meat and honeycomb back to the cow skin after it is done. (Note: add very little water as most meats have in-built liquids). Reduce heat to medium; add stockfish and smoked fish; simmer for view minutes together.

- Add tomato/pepper mixture, maggi or knorr cubes; mix and cook for 10-15 minutes; mix occasionally to avoid burning and to mix ingredients together. Add some water if soup appears thick.

- Add some broth from the soup into Egusi and mix in; then roll Egusi into tiny little balls and drop or sprinkle each one into the soup; cover and cook for twenty (20) minutes; occasionally mix prevent burning.

- Add crayfish and palm oil; cover and cook for 10 minutes or until soup is thick.

- Add vegetable; mix and simmer for another 5-10 minutes; stir occasionally.

- If soup appears dry or too thick, add water little by little and simmer for 5 minutes.

- Salt if needed to taste.

Serve soup with Eba, Amala, Iyan, Semolina or Fufu.

Assorted Meats: Goat meat, beef, chicken, turkey, beef oxtail, beef tripe, cow skin, cow legs, beef tripe, snail, stockfish, etc.

Vegetable Soup (Efo-Riro)

Ingredients:

2 16oz. bag Chopped Frozen Spinach	Fresh Ginger – to taste
1 small size stockfish – chopped	Fresh Garlic – to taste
2 pieces smoked or dried fish - shredded	3 habanera pepper (hot; adjust to taste)
1 tablespoon ground crayfish – optional	1 red bell pepper
3 tablespoon locust beans (Iru)	4 maggi or knorr cubes
1 15¼ oz. can tomato sauce	½ -1 cup palm oil or 1/3 cup of oil
2 - 3 tablespoon tomato paste	Water
1 medium onion	Salt to taste

Instructions:

Step 1

- Cover stockfish with water and boil with some salt until tender; set aside.

- Soak vegetable in salted water for 20 minutes; drain and remove excess water; set aside.

- Shred dried fish into small pieces and clean in hot water then soak in salted water for about twenty (20) minutes.

- Blend tomato sauce, paste, onion, ginger, garlic, habanera peppers, and red bell peppers; add little water during blending but enough for the blade to rotate; pour into a deep cooking pot and starting cooking on a medium high.

Step 2

- Add stockfish and smoked fish into tomato sauce mixture and cook for fifteen (15) minutes. Then add maggi or knorr cubes, crayfish; mix and cook for ten (10) minutes; mix occasionally to avoid burning.

- Reduce heat heat; add locust beans, palm oil and cook for ten (10) minutes. At this point, if soup appears watery cook soup longer; if it appears thick add water little by little till the right thickness attained.

- Add vegetable; mix thoroughly and simmer for another 5-10 minutes; stir occasionally.

- Salt if needed to taste.

Serve soup with Eba, Amala, Iyan, Semolina or Fufu.

Abak Atama Soup

This rich palm-nut soup is spiced and flavored with Atama leaves. Atama leaf can be used dried or fresh; the dried leaves are a lot more pungent in flavor. There are different variations of this soup.

Ingredients:

80 -100 bangas (fresh palm kernel seeds) or one can Trofia

8oz. dried Atama leaves – washed and shredded

1 small stockfish – chopped

1-1 ½ lbs. assorted meat - cut or cubes (see list below for assorted meat)

2 pieces smoked fish - shredded

1 cup Fresh shrimps

8oz. Periwinkle

2 tablespoon ground crayfish

1 medium onion

1 small Uyayak – local spice

1 tablespoon ground chili pepper (hot, adjust to taste)

4 maggi or knorr cubes

Water

Salt to taste

Instructions:

Step 1.

- Clean periwinkle very well to remove grits. Use lemon or lime juice to remove slime from the periwinkles; pre-cook or steam and set aside.

- In a deep pot, cover stockfish with water and boil with some salt until tender; set aside.

- Chop onion and set aside.

- Boil assorted meat with any meat seasoning until tender. (Add water if needed). Meat and honeycomb (tripe) will become tender before cow skin; so, remove these and continue cooking cow skin till tender or boil cow skin separately.

- Add meat, oxtail and honeycomb back to cow skin after it is done. Keep broth in.

Step 2.

Extracting palm oil from fresh palm kernel (Banga)

- Clean palm kernel and boil for 30 minutes or till nuts are soft. Remove Banga from cooking water and pour into a Mortar; pound with a pestle to separate the black seed, fiber, and the skin from the pulp.

- Add 4 cups of hot water and sieve through a colander (sifter) to drain out oil and palm kernel sauce into a deep cooking pot (discard the seed, fiber, and skin).

- Boil extracted palm oil for five minutes then

Step 3.

- Pour meat mixture, stockfish, smoked fish, periwinkles, chopped onion, ground chilies and knorr or maggi, Uyayak into the palm kernel oil and cook for 15 minutes. Mix occasionally to prevent burning.

If using Trafia

- Pour it into a deep cooking pot and thaw, then pour meat mixture, stockfish, smoked fish, periwinkles, onion, ground chilies, knorr or maggi, Uyayak and cook for 15 minutes. Mix occasionally to prevent burning.

- Reduce heat to medium and cook for ten (10) minutes or till the soup is fairly reduced and thickened to coat the back of the spoon. Occasionally mix soup.

- Add crayfish, shrimps and cook for ten (10) minutes at medium heat; then add Atama leaves and bring to boil for ten (10) minutes. Mix and add salt as needed to taste then simmer for five (5) minutes.

Serve soup over Rice or serve with Yan (pounded yam) or Fufu.

Assorted Meats: Goat meat, beef, chicken, smoked turkey, oxtail, beef tripe, cow skin, cow legs, beef tripe, snail, stockfish, etc.

Afang/Okazi/Ukazi Soup

Afang Soup is a traditional Nigerian stew from South-Eastern part of the country (Akwa Ibom, Igbos, and Cross River State). There are different variations of this soup; especially the type of meat and fish options.

Instructions:

2 pounds Afang leaves - cleaned and chopped

1 pound Waterleaf (cleaned and chopped) or 16 oz. bag chopped frozen Spinach

1 lb. assorted meat – diced

1 small stockfish - cut or chopped

1 cup periwinkles - cleaned

1 cup dried prawn - chopped

2 pieces dried fish – shredded

2 tablespoon ground crayfish

1 onion - chopped

2 hot chili Pepper - hot adjust to taste

1 cup palm oil

4 Knorr or Maggi cubes

Water

Salt to taste

Instructions:

Step 1.

- In a deep pot, cover stockfish with water and boil with some salt until tender; set aside.

- Rinse and drain Afang leaves to get rid of sediment; chopped and set aside.

- Soak Chopped Spinach in salted water for about 20 minutes; drain and set aside.

- Shred dried fish into small pieces and clean in hot water. Set aside.

- Clean periwinkles with lemon or lime juice very well to get rid of sand and grits that come with periwinkles naturally or follow clean direction on the package. Per-boil periwinkles with very little water and salt. Set aside.

Step 2.

- Boil assorted meat with little salt till tender (add water if needed) then, add boiled stockfish and simmer for five (5) minutes.

- Add periwinkles, dried fish, crayfish, waterleaves or chopped Spinach, pepper, onion and knorr or maggi and cook all for ten (10) minutes at medium heat; mix thoroughly and occasionally to prevent burning.

- Add chopped Afang leaves; crushed dried prawns, palm oil; cover and cook for fifteen (15) minutes at medium heat or till greens are soft and tender. Also to bring all the flavors together. If soup appears dry or thick add very little water at a time; add salt if needed to taste.

Serve soup with Iyan (Pounded yam, Fufu, and Eba.

These ingredients can be purchased from your local African grocery store.

1. **Afang/Ukazi/Okazi leaves** are all the same. Afang leaves are an ingredient in the popular Igbo dish. As mentioned above, the Calabar, Efik and Ibibios call it Afang, while Igbos call it Ukazi/Okazi.

2. **Periwinkles** are form of snails. They are much smaller than typical snails and can be described as tiny snails. As with regular snails, they need to be thoroughly cleaned to get rid of grit and dirt from their natural habitat. You can purchase them at your local African grocery store. They can be purchased already out of shell but still need to be clean very well or the soup would be totally ruined with sand and grits.

3. Periwinkles are also known as **Ishan in Yoruba** with different variations in spelling.

4. **Waterleaves** are also known as "**Gbure**" in Yoruba.

Assorted Meats: Goat meat, beef, chicken, turkey, beef oxtail, beef tripe, cow skin, cow legs, beef tripe, snail, and stockfish etc.

Banga Soup (Palm Kernel Soup)

This Soup is made from Palm Kernel Fruit (Elaeis Guineensis).

Ingredients:

80 -100 bangas (fresh palm kernel) seeds

1 10oz. chopped Okra – chopped into tiny pieces

1 small stockfish – chopped

1 lb. assorted meat - cut or cubes (see list below for assorted)

2 tablespoon ground Crayfish

2 pieces dried fish - shredded

1 tablespoon Ugu (Bitter leaf) - optional

1 medium onion

1 tablespoon ground hot red pepper (adjust to taste)

4 maggi or knorr cubes

3 – 4 cups water

Salt to taste

Instructions:

Step 1

- In a deep pot, cover stockfish with water and boil with some salt until tender; set aside.

- Shred dried fish into small pieces and clean with hot water. Set aside.

- Chop onion and set aside.

- Chop Okra and set aside.

- Boil assorted meat with any meat seasoning until tender. (Add water if needed). Meat and honeycomb (tripe) will become tender before cow skin; so, remove these and continue cooking cow skin until tender or boil the cow skin separately.

- Add meat, honeycomb back to the cow skin after it is done. Add water if need and keep broth in it.

Step 2

Extracting palm oil from fresh palm kernel (Banga):

- Clean palm kernel and boil for 30 minutes or until soft and tender.

- Remove from cooking water and pour into a Mortar; pound with a pestle to separate the black seed, fiber, and the skin from the pulp. Add 4 cups of the hot water and sieve through a colander (sifter) to drain out oil and palm kernel source into a deep cooking pot (discard the seed, fiber, and skin) and boil for five minutes.

Step 3

- Add meat mixture into the extracted palm oil; stockfish, dried fish, chopped onion, red hot pepper and knorr or maggi; then cook for 15 minutes.

- Add Ugu (bitter leaf) and ground crayfish; mix and reduce heat to medium; occasionally stir soup to allow ingredients to mix evenly.

- Cook for 15 minutes until the soup is fairly reduced and thickened to coat the back of the spoon. Now add Chopped Okra and cook for another ten (10) minutes.

- Add very little water if soup appears thick or cook longer to thicken the soup.

- Add salt as needed.

Serve with Iyan (pounded Yam), Eba, Semolina or Fufu.

Assorted Meats: Goat meat, beef, chicken, turkey, beef oxtail, beef tripe, cow skin, cow leg, beef tripe, snail, stockfish, etc.

Edikang Ikong Soup

This vegetable soup is very rich and delicious. It is commonly served as a delicacy during very special ceremonies. According to some people, few people know how to cook the soup.

Ingredients:

3 lbs. fresh Ugu/pumpkin leaves –washed and shredded

2 10 oz. Frozen Spinach or Waterleaf

6 Snails – cleaned

1 small stockfish - Chopped

2 lbs. assorted meat - Beef, oxtail, tripe, cow leg, cow skin and chicken gizzard - diced

2 pieces dry fish

4 pieces crabs - cut the body into 2 pieces each.

1lb. periwinkles – top & tail – cleaned

2 tablespoon whole dry Prawns – cleaned

2 tablespoon ground crayfish

1 medium onion

1 tablespoon hot pepper

1 - 2 cups palm oil

4 - 6 maggi or knorr cubes

2 - 4 cups of water

Salt to taste

Instructions:

Step 1.

- Clean periwinkles very well to remove grits. Use lemon or lime juice to remove slime from the periwinkles; set aside.

- Remove the snails from shells and clean thoroughly to remove grits; use lime or lemon juice again to remove slime. Set aside.

- Clean crabs thoroughly and divide into two each. Combine periwinkles, snails, and crabs and boil with salt; set aside.

- Clean dry fish; drain and add to crabs/snails mixture.

- Boil chicken gizzard and add to meat mixture.

- In a deep pot, cover stockfish with water and boil with some salt until tender; add to meat mixture.

- Boil assorted meat with any meat seasoning and onion until tender. (Add water if needed). Meat and honeycomb (tripe) will become tender before cow skin; so, remove these and continue cooking cow skin until tender or boil the cow skin separately.

- Combine all the meat, gizzard, periwinkles, snails, crabs, prawns, pepper, knorr or maggi and simmer for 15 minutes at medium heat. Add more water if need and the keep broth.

Step 2.

- Add shredded Ugwu/pumpkin leaves and Spinach or Waterleaf; mix thoroughly and cook for 15 minutes; stir in between to avoid burning the soup; then add crayfish and palm oil; mix and reduce heat to medium; simmer for about 15-20 minutes. Add more water as needed if soup appears too thick and salt if needed to taste.

Serve Soup with Iyan (pounded Yam), Eba, Amala, Semolina, or Fufu.

Assorted Meats: Goat meat, beef, chicken, smoked turkey, oxtail, beef tripe, cow skin, cow legs, beef tripe, snail, stockfish, etc.

Epe Crab Soup

Experimentations lead to new taste discoveries. The case of Deji's experimentation with Epe Crab Soup is one successful example.

Ingredients:

Fresh crabs steamed and cleaned.

Normal ingredients for your favorite Nigerian soup.

Instructions:

Cook your favorite soup as usual, but substitute crabs for the usual meat of fish options. A similar experimentation can be done with cooked chicken feet, gizzards, and other assorted parts. Even shrimp can be a decent substitute.

Deji's Lagosian Crab Soup

She Crabs laden with egg make very eggcellent soup. This soup is popularly known as "Obe Imoyo" (Imoyo soup) in the local Yoruba dialect of Lagos. Indigenes of Lagos (Lagosians) serve Imoyo soup with eba (garri), fufu, or pounded yam. Substitutes for imoyo soup include okro soup, or egusi soup.

Lagos, being a coastal city, affords her residents a staple food of she-crab soup. This was very prevalent in the 1950s, 060s, and 70s. The urbanization of most of the coastal areas of Lagos island has decimated the traditional crab habitats, where we used to hunt and grab crabs when we were growing up in Lagos. You will have to look far and wide before you can find and catch fresh crabs yourself in Lagos these days. Of course, you can always go to the market to buy commercial crabs. An easy way out!

Ingredients:

Chopped onions (small-sized)

Chopped chili pepper, one tablespoon

Chopped garlic (one clove)

Vinegar 1 teaspoon

Olive oil 1 table-spoon

Directions:

1. Cover crabs with boiling water and cook for 20 minutes.

2. Add all seasoning and simmer for 10 minutes in a saucepan.

3. Remove outer shell from crabs (if you desire, you remove flesh from the claws and body cavity of the crabs).

4. Use crab meat and parts as insert in your favorite soup (e.g., okra soup, egusi soup, etc.).

5. Serve with hot fufu (e.g., Eba, Amala, etc.)

Gbegiri Soup (Beans Soup)

Ingredients:

1lb. bag blackeye peas or African red beans

1 large dried fish (shredded)

½ tablespoon ground crayfish

½ tablespoon red hot pepper (adjust to taste)

1 medium onion - chopped

1/3 cup palm oil

3 maggi or knorr cubes - crushed

6 - 8 cups of Water

Salt to taste

Instructions:

Step 1

Cleaning the beans

- Soak blackeye peas in cold water for about five minutes. (This will allow the beans to swell up and make it easy to remove the outer coat); or pour small amount of the beans into the blender, cover with water; grind for about 3 – 5 seconds (do not blend) and pour the beans into a large bowl; continue the process until finish.

- Cover beans with water; rub beans in between palms of both hands back and forth in the water to loosen the outer coat. The outer coat will naturally float to the top.

- Use a strainer to separate beans from the outer coat by draining the floating coats. Continue this process until beans is cleaned and no more coats or dark sport. Filter and change water as many times as needed.

- Shred dried fish into tiny pieces and wash in hot water to remove any sand; set aside.

Cooking

- Combine beans, onion, 6-8 cups of water and cook in a deep cooking pot until very soft and tender.

- Mash beans until it turns into puree but not watery; then add shredded dried fish, pepper, ground crayfish, maggi or knorr; cook for ten (10) minutes. Mix soup during cooking to avoid burning. If soup appears watery, cook longer and if thick add little water.

- Add palm oil and continue cooking for ten (10) minutes.

- Reduce heat to low and simmer for ten (10) minutes; stir soup intermittently to prevent sticking to the bottom of the pot or burning.

- Salt as needed to taste.

Serve with Tuwo, Amala or Fufu with any meat stew on top.

Miya Tanse Soup

Ingredients:

1 lb. meat – cut or diced

1 lb. smoked meat – cut or diced

1 16 oz. bag Spinach

2 medium size fresh tomatoes - chopped

1 medium onion – chopped

2 pieces chili pepper - chopped

1 cup groundnut - blend

3 maggi or knorr cubes

Water

Oil

Salt to taste

Instructions:

Step 1

- Boil meat and smoked meat with seasoning until tender. Set aside.

- Soak spinach in salted water for 15 minutes; drain and set aside.

- In a cooking pot, add some oil, fry chopped onion, tomatoes and pepper then add boiled meat, maggi and continue cooking for ten (10) minutes. Add little water if needed.

- Add groundnut and cook for 15 minutes.

- Add smoked meat, vegetable and simmer for ten (10) minutes. Add salt if needed to taste.

Serve with Tuwo

Ofe-Owerri Soup

This is a classic Oweri soup flavored with aromatic Uzouza leaves and lightly thickened with Cocoyam. There are different variations of this soup, based on the type of meats, vegetables, and fish used.

Ingredients:

16 oz. Okazi/Ukazi leaves – shredded and cleaned

1 cup Ugu/pumpkin leaves or 1 10oz. bag Collard greens

1 lb. cocoyam - boiled and pounded to soft paste

1 ½ lbs. assorted meat – cow skin, oxtail, honeycomb, tripe (shaki) –cut or cubes

1 small stockfish – cut or chopped

2 pieces smoked fish – shredded

6 pieces snail

1lb. periwinkles – cleaned

8oz. dry Prawns – cleaned

1 tbsp. ground hot pepper – adjust to taste

2 Tbsp. ground dried crayfish

1 onion

3 - 4 maggi or knorr cubes

1 cup palm oil

Water

Salt to taste

Instructions:

- If using Collard greens and Chopped spinach, thaw and soak in salted water for about 20 minutes; drain and set aside.

- Wash cocoyam and peel; cook till soft; drain left over water and pound to form paste. Set aside.

- Shred dried fish into small pieces and clean in hot water. Set aside.

- Clean snails and periwinkles very well to remove grits. Use lemon or lime juice to remove slime; per-boil and set aside.

- Cover stockfish with water and boil with some salt until tender; add to snail mixture.

- Boil assorted meat with any meat seasoning and onion until tender. (Add water if needed). Meat and honeycomb (tripe) will become tender before cow skin; so, remove these and continue cooking the cow skin until tender or boil the cow skin separately.

- Add meat, oxtail and honeycomb back to the cow skin; add snail/stockfish mixture, dried fish, dry Prawns, pepper and knorr or maggi; simmer all for about 10 - 15 minutes.

- Now form the pounded cocoyam into small balls and add to the soup; mix thoroughly.

- Add crayfish palm oil and simmer for 20 minutes.

- Now add shredded Okazi/Ukazi leaves, Ugu/pumpkin leaves; cover and cook at medium heat for 10 minutes or till greens are tender. Mix thoroughly and occasionally to prevent burning.

- Add salt to taste if needed.

Serve soup with Iyan (pounded yam), Eba or Fufu.

Assorted Meats: Goat meat, beef, chicken, smoked turkey, oxtail, beef tripe, cow skin, cow legs, beef tripe, snail, and stockfish etc.

Oha/Ora Soup

This is a very traditional soup and similar to bitter leaf soup, but cooked with tender Ora leaves.

Ingredients:

16 oz. Oha/Ora leaves – chopped leaves with hand to prevent from getting dark in color

6 Cocoyams

1 small stockfish - chopped

1 ½ lbs. assorted beef – Goat meat, tripe and cow skin - cut or diced

2 pieces dried fish - shredded

1 tablespoon ground crayfish

1 tablespoon ground hot red pepper

1 tablespoon iru or ogiri – optional (local spice)

3 maggi or knorr cubes

½ - 1 cup palm oil

Salt to taste

Instructions:

- Wash, peel and cook cocoyam till very soft; pound to a smooth paste and set aside.

- In a deep pot, cover stockfish with water and boil with some salt until tender; set aside.

- Cut or diced meat; boil with onion and little salt until tender; remove excess broth from the meat and replace with water; add stockfish and cook for five (5) minutes.

- Add crayfish, dried fish, pepper, iru/ogiri, maggi and cook for ten (10) minutes. Occasionally stir soup to prevent burning and to allow ingredients to mix evenly.

- Add cocoyam paste in small lumps; palm oil; cover and cook till all the cocoyam lumps have dissolved. Add more water if soup appears too thick little by little.

- Add Ora leaves and simmer for ten (10) minutes.

- Add salt if needed to taste.

Serve with Eba, Fufu, Semolina or Amala.

Ottong Soup

Instructions:

1 ½ lbs. assorted meat - cut or cubes

1 small stockfish

2 pieces smoked or dried fish

1 lb. periwinkle (remove the shell)

1 cup shrimps - optional

2 tablespoons ground crayfish

1 10oz. bag Okra - chopped

¼ cup Blended Ogbono

8oz. Ugwu/pumpkin leaves

1tablespoon ground hot red pepper (adjust to taste)

1 medium onion - chopped

½ - 1 cup palm oil

4 maggi or knorr cubes

Water

Salt to taste

Instructions:

Step 1

- Chop Okra (not blend); set aside.

- Wash, shred, and soak Ugwu/pumpkin leaves for about 15 - 20 minutes in salted water; drain and set aside.

- Shred smoked dried fish into small pieces and wash in hot water. Set aside.

- Clean periwinkle very well to remove grits. Use lemon or lime juice to remove slime from the periwinkles; set aside.

- Thaw shrimps and set aside.

- Cover stockfish with water and boil with some salt until tender; set aside.

- Boil assorted meat seasoning until tender (add water if needed). Meat and honeycomb (tripe) will become tender before cow skin; so, remove these and continue cooking cow skin until tender or boil cow skin separately.

- Add meat, and honeycomb back to the cow skin after it is done; reduce heat and add stockfish, smoked fish, periwinkle, pepper, onion, maggi or knorr cubes and about 2-3 cups of water if needed or broth in the meat may be enough; simmer for ten (10) minutes; reduce heat to low to get Ogbono ready.

- Step 2 Preparing Ogbono

- In a small cooking pot, add half the palm oil and heat a little; reduce heat to medium; stir in Apon/ Ogbono slowly and stir constantly as you add Ogbono; fry for two (2) minutes (do not over try or burn). Reduce heat if necessary.

- Stir in two (2) cups of water (as you stir in the water, Apon/Agbono will rise up and draw). Continue stirring until a smooth consistency is obtained and lump free. Cook for ten (10) minutes at medium heat. If Ogbono appears thick, add little water **or in steady of using palm oil, bring one cup of water to boil; stir in Ogbono slowly and stir constantly; as you add, Ogbono will rise up and draw; continue stirring until a smooth consistency is obtained and lump free; then add two (2) cups of and cook for ten (10) minutes.**

- Add Ogbono to meat/stockfish mixture and mix thoroughly; add ground crayfish, shrimps and cook for another fifteen (15) minutes. Stir occasionally during cooking to prevent burning.

- Add Ugwu/pumpkin leaves and cook for ten (10) minutes or till vegetable soft; add chopped Okra and allow to bubble for five (5) minutes.

- Add salt and little water if needed; then cook for 5 minutes.

Serve soup with Eba, Amala, Iyan, Semolina or Fufu.

There are different variations of this soup, depending on the type of meats, fish, or sea food options used.

Assorted Meats: Goat meat, beef, chicken, smoked turkey, oxtail, beef tripe, cow skin, cow legs, beef tripe, snail, stockfish, etc.

Rice and Tripe (or shrimp) Combo

Ingredients:

1 pound shrimp

4 – 5 pieces crabs – cut into 2 each

1 large onion – chopped

2 clove garlic – chopped

1 large green bell pepper – chopped

2 28-oz. can tomato

1 16-oz. can tomato sauce

1 cup red wine

1 bay leaf

1 teaspoon basil

½ teaspoon oregano leaves

¼ cup olive oil

Instructions:

- Clean and boil crabs; set aside.

- In a frying pan or saucepan, sauté onion, garlic and green bell pepper in olive oil.

- Add tomato, tomato sauce, wine, bay leaf, basil and oregano; mix well and bring to boil; reduce heat and simmer for 20 minutes.

- Add crab and shrimp; cover and simmer ten (10) minutes; remove bay leaf and discard

- Serve hot over rice.

Ukpo Soup

This very rich Okra and vegetable soup is from the South-East region of Nigeria. There are different variations of it, depending on the type of meats, fish or sea food selections.

Ingredients:

4 Ukpo Seeds

1 small stockfish - chopped

½ lb. Smoked Turkey – chopped or diced

1 lb. beef - diced

8oz. Okazi

4oz. dried fish

1 tablespoon ground crayfish

2 tablespoon dadawa or Iru

½ tbsp. ground hot red pepper

3-4 maggi or knorr cubes

½ cup palm oil

Salt to taste

Instructions:

Step 1

- Crack Ukpo seeds and boil for 1 ½ hours or until soft and tender.

- Pour hot Ukpo into a Mortar and Pound with a pestle; add some palm oil and pound until it is powdery. Set aside.

- In a deep pot, cover stockfish with water and boil with some salt until tender; set aside.

- Cut or diced meat; boil with onion and two (2) maggi or knorr cubes until tender; keep broth in it and set aside.

- Wash smoked Turkey in warm water first, then add to meat; add stockfish and cook for 10 minutes at medium heat.

- Add crayfish, dried fish, dadawa (Iru), palm oil, remaining maggi if needed and pepper; cook for another ten (10) minutes. Occasionally stir soup to prevent burning and to allow ingredients to mix evenly. If needed add about ½ to one cup of water; mix and cook for five (5) minutes.

- Add Ukpo, mix and cook 10 minutes covered; add Okazi and cook for another five (5) minutes.

- Add salt if needed to taste.

White Soup/NSala

Ingredients:

1 Big Fresh Cat Fish – clean and cut into small sizes

3 pieces sliced Yam or ½ cup Yam Flour – as thickner

1 tablespoon Crayfish

1 tablespoon Ogiri

2 habanera pepper – Blend (optional)

1 medium onion

1 tablespoon cleaned Utazi or bitter leaf

3 maggi or knorr cubes

8 -10 cups of water

Salt to taste

Instructions:

- Clean and cut cat fish into small – medium size pieces; add boil water, this will harden the pieces of fish and will not dissolve while cooking.

- Dice pieces of sliced yam and boil yam till soft; pound to form a smooth paste **or** mix yam flour with cold water to get smooth thick paste. Set aside

- Combine eight (8) cups of water, blended habanera, Utazi or bitter leaf, chopped onion, maggi or knorr cubes and cook for ten (10) minutes.

- Add cat fish, crayfish and ogiri; cover and cook for 15 minutes at medium high; stir intermittently to allow ingredients to mix evenly and to avoid burning.

- Add yam paste in small lumps; cover and allow the soup to cook and bubble, the yam past should dissolve.

- If the soup appears too thick, add more water. It should not be too thick or too thin; add salt to taste. Enjoy!

Serve with Eba, Amala, Fufu or Semolina.

Spicy Mixed Pepper Soup with Bitter Leaf

Ingredients:

3 lb. assorted meat (beef tripe, cow skin, beef kidney and goat meat or beef)

2 tablespoon pepper soup seasoning

3 habanera – chopped (hot adjust to taste)

1 large onion

2 tablespoon crayfish

1 tablespoon bitter leaf

3 maggi or knorr cubes

8 -10 cups of water

Instructions:

Step 1

- Dice assorted meat; boil with onion, knorr or maggi cubes until tender and soft (keep stock).

- Add six (6) cups of water, pepper soup seasoning, crayfish, bitter leaf, habanera and simmer for 20 - 25 minutes. Occasionally, stir soup to prevent burning and also to allow ingredients to mix evenly.

- Add more water in needed and salt to taste.

Pepper Soup seasonings are mixture of local herbs and spices and are not readily available in most supermarkets except in stores specializing in African Foods.

Cat Fish Pepper Soup

Ingredients:

1 Big Fresh Cat Fish – cut into small sizes

1 tablespoon pepper soup seasoning

2 habanera – chopped (hot adjust to taste)

1 large onion

1 tablespoon bitterleaf

3 maggi or knorr cubes

8 -10 cups of water

Instructions:

Step 1.

- Combine eight (8) cups of water, pepper soup seasoning, bitter leaf, habanera, chopped onion, maggi or knorr cubes and simmer for 20 - 25 minutes.

- Add cat fish, cover and cook for 15 minutes and medium high; lower heat to low and simmer for five (5) minutes. Occasionally, stir to allow ingredients to mix evenly.

- Add salt to taste.

Pepper Soup seasonings are mixture of local herbs and spices and are not readily available in most supermarkets except in stores specializing in African Foods.

Isi-Ewu (Goat Head Pepper Soup)

Ingredients:

1 Goat head and legs – clean & cut into small pieces	3 teaspoon Lemon juice
3 habanera peppers – hot, adjust to taste	1 tbsp. pepper soup seasoning
5 fresh tomatoes	1 tbsp. Ugu - Bitter leaf
2 small onions – chopped	4 maggi or knorr cubes
4 tablespoon tomato paste	½ cup palm oil
2 clove garlic	8 - 10 cups water
Some ginger – optional	Salt to taste

Instructions:

- Blend fresh tomato, habanera peppers, onion, ginger, garlic, and ginger and tomato paste. Set aside.

- Clean goat head and the legs very well to remove any grits and hair then cut into small pieces; remove any parts that you do not want; add lemon juice, mix and marinate for about 20 minutes.

- In a large deep cooking pot, add goat head, eight (8) cups of water, two (2) maggi or knorr cubes and cook until soft and tender; add more water if needed. Reduce heat to medium heat.

- Add tomato/pepper mixture, ugu (better leaf), pepper soup seasoning, remaining maggi cover and cook for 20 minutes. Mix occasionally to prevent burning; add palm oil and simmer for another 15 minutes at low heat.

- Add salt to taste and water if needed to thin out soup.

Serve hot.

Spicy Goat Legs Pepper Soup

Ingredients:

12 pieces goat leg or cow leg

3 habanera peppers - hot, adjust to taste

1 medium onions - sliced

2 clove garlic - chopped

Some ginger - chopped

1 tablespoon ground crayfish

1 tablespoon bitter leaf

4 maggi or knorr cubes

½ cup palm oil

6 – 8 cups water

Salt to taste

Instructions:

- Clean goat/cow legs very well to remove any grits and hair.

- In a large deep cooking pot, add goat legs and cook till tender with some maggi or knorr and salt. Set aside.

- Combine chopped onion, pepper, chopped garlic, ginger, crayfish, maggi or knorr and six (6) cups of water. Mix and cook for ten (10) minutes. Mix occasionally to prevent burning; add palm oil and simmer for another ten (10) minutes. Add more water if thinner soup is choice and for thicker soup use cocoyam flour as thickener.

- Add goat legs; bitter leaf; reduce heat to low and simmer for 15 minutes.

Serve hot.

Baked Rice

Ingredients:

5 cups uncooked rice

6 cups of water

1 small onion – finely chopped

¼ cup celery – finely chopped

¼ cup finely chopped green and red bell peppers

¼ cup olive oil or butter

½ teaspoon garlic powder

Salt to taste

Instructions:

- In a deep cooking pot add oil or butter; add rice and stir fry until golden brown (stir constantly to avoid burning); add six (6) cups of water to per-boil rice for about ten (10) minutes.

- Turn the heat off; add chopped onion, celery, bell peppers and garlic powder; mix and add salt to taste.

- Pour rice into a 9 X 13-inch baking dish; cover with foil; bake at 350 degrees for fifty (50) minutes or until rice is cooked.

Note: serve with baked chicken, fish or steak.

Coconut Rice

Ingredients:

4 cups of Rice	½ tablespoon ground pepper or to taste
5 cups coconut milk	2 - 3 pieces carrots - diced
1 lb. boneless chicken - diced	1 medium onion - chopped
1 lb. shrimp	1/4 cup oil
1 cup peas	4 maggi or knorr cubes
1 tablespoon ground crayfish or to taste	Water
2 red bell peppers – diced	Salt to taste
2 medium size fresh tomatoes – diced	

Instructions:

Step 1

- Using fresh coconut fruit: crack 2 coconuts open; remove the white flesh and roughly grate;

- Pour hot water to cover grated coconut and leave to stand for about 30 minutes.

- Remove the roughage by press and squeeze the flesh to extract the milk; then sieve the liquid to remove any leftover roughage. (The more water one uses, the thinner the milk will be). In general, on fresh coconut will yield about 2 cups of milk **or** use two cans of coconut milk.

- Parboil rice and set aside.

- Dice chicken and boil with little water; add onion and maggi or knorr until tender; add shrimp and steam for about 5 minutes; Set aside.

- Boil coconut milk for about ten (10) minutes at medium heat; add rice and cook till rice is almost done. Add water if needed.

- Add chicken/shrimp mixture; diced tomatoes, pepper and oil; reduce heat to low, cover and simmer till rice is done and the liquid is absorbed. However, if water is needed add little by little. **Note: do not add too much water or the rice will be mushy or soggy.**

- Add diced carrots, peas, red bell pepper; mix and steam for view minutes. Add salt to taste if needed.

Serve with Dodo, Moin-Moin any vegetable. For Meat: Baked Chicken, Fried Chicken, Baked Fish, Fried Fish or Steak. Enjoy.

Fried Rice Platter

There are many variations of fried rice, each with its own specific ingredients. A good example is the friend rice platter with a variety of toppings and garnishings.

Ingredients:

4 cups Rice	4 maggi or knorr cubes - crushed
1 lb. Shrimp	1 teaspoon thyme
1 cup cooked chicken gizzards – diced into tiny pieces	1 teaspoon curry
1 10oz. pkg. frozen peas & carrots	1 cup oil or butter
1 large onion - diced	Water
Garlic - to taste (chopped)	Salt to taste

Instructions:

- Clean, dice and boil gizzards with onion and some maggi or knorr until tender; set aside

- Drain water out of shrimp and peas/carrot vegetable. Set them aside.

- Add oil or butter into a deep cooking pot and heat over medium heat; add garlic and stir fry for one minute; add rice; stir fry (stir continuously to avoid burning) for about 10 minutes or till rice is brown (not burn).

- Add 6 cups of water, remaining maggi or knorr cubes(if needed), thyme, curry, sliced onion, mix thoroughly, (if water is needed, add ½ to one cup); cover and steam for 15 minutes or until rice is almost done. **Note: do not add too much water or the rice will be mushy or soggy.**

- Open and stir rice; add boiled gizzard; shrimp, vegetable, mix and steam for another 10 – 15 minutes or until rice is cooked; taste to see if rice is done.

- Add salt to taste if needed.

Serve with: Dodo, Moin-Moin, Beans, and vegetable. Meat: Baked Chicken, Fried Chicken, Baked Fish, Fried Fish or Steak.

Jollof Rice

Jollof rice is common in many African countries. Each country, seems to have its own twist to the jollof rice craze. There is even an active debate on which country has the best jollof rice. Senegal is said to be the birthplace of jollof rice, but Ghana and Nigeria will dispute that.

Ingredients:

4 cups Rice	4 maggi or knorr cubes
1 15oz. can tomato sauce	1/4 teaspoon curry powder
2 large fresh tomatoes	1/4 teaspoon ground thyme
1 6oz. can tomato paste	5 pieces bay leaves
1 medium onion	½ cup of oil
3 habanera peppers (hot, adjust to taste)	Water
2 red bell peppers	Salt to taste
Garlic to taste	

Instructions:

- Blend tomato sauce, fresh tomatoes, paste, onion, garlic, habanera peppers, and red bell peppers together. Add very little water as needed during blending for the blade to rotate.

- Pour blended tomato/pepper mixture into a deep cooking pot; add maggi or knorr cubes, thyme, curry; six (6) cups of water, cook for 15 minutes at medium heat. Mix and stir occasionally during cooking to mix ingredients evenly.

- Reduce heat to low heat; wash rice and rinse to remove excess starch; add rice to tomato/pepper mixture; mix thoroughly; add oil, bay leaves; mix and cover; steam until all the liquid is absorbed into the rice.

- Open and taste rice to see if it is done. If not, add about ½ cup water as needed; mix; cover and simmer for another 10 - 15 minutes. Add water as needed little by little if rice is still hard. **Note: do not add too much water or the rice will be mushy or soggy.**

- Open and stir rice thoroughly to prevent from sticking together or burning then simmer for 5 minutes. Add salt if needed.

Serve with: Dodo, Moin-Moin, any green vegetables. Meat: Baked Chicken, Fried Chicken, Baked Fish, Fried Fish or Steak.

Rice and Beans Porridge

Ingredients:

2 cups Rice

1 lb. bag blackeye peas or African Red Beans

1 15oz. can of tomato sauce

3 tbsp. tomato paste

1 medium onion

2 habanera peppers (hot, adjust to taste)

1 red bell pepper

2 clove garlic

3 maggi or knorr cubes

¼ teaspoon curry powder

½ cup palm oil or 1/3 cup oil

6-8 cups of water

Salt to taste

Instructions:

- Blend tomato sauce, paste, onion, garlic, habanera peppers, and red bell pepper together. Add very little water as needed during blending for the blade to rotate. Set aside.

- Soak blackeye peas in cold water for about five minutes. (This will allow the beans to swell up and make it easy to remove the outer coat); or pour small amount of the beans into the blender, cover with water; grind for about 3 – 5 seconds (do not blend) and pour the beans into a large bowl; continue the process until finish.

- Cover beans with water; rub beans in between palms of both hands back and forth in the water to loosen the outer coat. The outer coat will naturally float to the top.

- Use a strainer to separate beans from the outer coat by draining the floating coats. Continue this process until beans is cleaned and no more coats or dark sport. Filter and change water as many times as needed.

- Pour cleaned bean into a deep cooking pot; cover with water and cook on medium high heat for 20 minutes. Cook the bean half way done.

- Wash rice and rinse to remove excess starch; add to cooking beans; mix; cover and cook together for 15 – 20 minutes. Reduce heat if needed to prevent burning. Also you may need to add more water to the beans and rice if all the liquid is absorbed into the porridge while rice or beans still hard.

- Add tomato/pepper mixture, maggi or knorr cubes, thyme, curry, palm oil; mix, cover and cook for 15 minutes or until porridge is cooked at low heat to avoid burning. Also Stir porridge intermittently and continue simmering for ten (10) minutes.

- Add salt if needed.

Rice and Chicken Casserole

Ingredients:

2 lbs. boneless chicken breast – remove skin and dice

1 10¾ oz. can condensed cream of mushroom

1 10¾ oz. can condensed cream of broccoli or celery

1 medium onion – dice

2 tablespoon olive oil or butter

2 14½ oz. can French style green beans rinse and drain

1 4oz. jar pimentos

1 cup uncooked rice

1½ - 2 cup grated cheddar cheese

Salt to taste

Instructions:

- Preheat oven to 350 degrees F.

- Clean and dice the chicken; per boil with a pinch of salt for about five (5) minutes. (do not add water)

- Heat oil or butter in a frying pan over medium heat; add onion, pinch of salt, and sauté for five (5) minutes.

- Remove from heat and transfer to a large bowl; add all the remaining ingredients except cheese; mix all together until thoroughly mixed.

- Pour into a greased large casserole baking dish or pan; baked for 25-30 minutes or until bubbly; add cheese and bake for 10 minutes.

Rice with Goat Meat and Chicken Curry

Ingredients:

1 lb. boneless goat meat - diced

1 lb. boneless chicken - diced

1 can 15 oz. diced tomatoes - on drained

1 medium onion - chopped

1 medium red bell pepper – chopped

1 medium green bell pepper – chopped

2 tablespoon curry powder – adjust to your taste

2 habaneras pepper – hot, adjust to taste (optional)

1 cup chopped carrot

2 maggi cubes

Salt to taste

Rise - cook for about six (6)

Instructions:

- Clean and boil meat and chicken with maggi cubes; add little water as most meat produces water as it cooks; drain and excess broth.

- Combine meat/chicken, tomatoes, chopped onion, red and green bell peppers, carrot, habanera, and curry powder; mix and bring to a boil; reduce heat to low; cover and simmer for 45 minutes. Stir periodically.

- Add salt to taste

Serve over hot cook rice and serve.

Lemon Chicken and Rice

Ingredients:

4 chicken breast halves

8 pieces potatoes

1 medium red bell pepper - diced

1 medium red onion - chopped

8-oz. whole mushrooms - sliced

2 lemons – divided

¼ cup olive oil

4 large garlic cloves – chopped

2-3 teaspoon dried oregano leaves

½ teaspoons coarsely ground black pepper

Salt to taste

Instructions:

Step 1.

- Using lemon zester, zest one lemon to measure 1½ tablespoons.

- Juice lemon to measure one tablespoon juice.

- In a mixing bowl, combine lemon zest, juice, oil, garlic (pressed), oregano, salt and black pepper; mix well.

- Arrange chicken in a baking pan; brush chicken with a portion of the lemon juice mixture.

- Scrub potatoes well and pat dry and cut potatoes in half; slice remaining lemon.

- In a mixing bowl, combine potatoes, bell pepper, onion, lemon slices and mushrooms with remaining lemon juice mixture; toss to coat.

- Arrange vegetables around chicken in the baking pan.

- Preheat oven to 400 degrees F.

- Bake for 30 minutes, then brush chicken and vegetables with the juice in the pan all over; bake for another 30 minutes or until chicken is done.

Serve over rice.

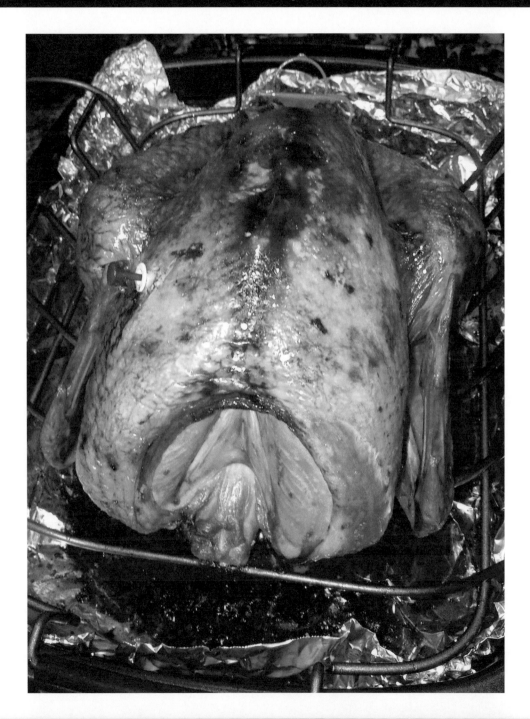

Mushroom and Rice

Ingredients:

4-5 cups cooked Rice	2 cups milk
1lbs. mushroom – sliced	Salt and pepper
1 onion – chopped	Pinch cayenne pepper
2 tablespoon oil	3 tablespoon chopped fresh parsley
¼ lb. butter	½ cup dry bread crumbs
3 tablespoon flour	¼ cup grated Parmesan cheese

Directions:

- In a large frying pan, sauté onion and mushrooms with three (3) tablespoons of butter for about 15 minutes.

- Add another three (3) tablespoons butter and stir until melted.

- Stir in flour until smooth; gradually stir in milk; add some salt, ½ teaspoon pepper and cayenne.

- Bring to a boil and cook for two (2) minute; add rice and two (2) tablespoon parsley; mix and pour mixture into a 2-qt casserole pan; top with cheese and bake at 350 degrees.

Asaro (Yam Porridge)

Ingredients:

1 Large Yam	1tablespoon ground crayfish
1 15oz. can tomato sauce	3 maggi or knorr cubes
3 tablespoon tomato paste	3 tablespoon brown or white sugar - adjust to taste
1 medium onion	½ cup palm oil or 1/3 oil
2 habaneras or chili peppers (hot, adjust to taste)	Water
2 red bell peppers	½ teaspoon salt
Garlic to taste	

Instructions:

- Blend tomato sauce, tomato paste, onion, garlic, habanera peppers, and red bell peppers. Add enough water for the blade to rotate during blending; set aside.

- Peel yam; slice into small pieces; wash in cold water and pour into a deep cooking pot.

- Add 3 cups of water, salt, and brown sugar; cover and cook yam until almost cook and reduce heat to low heat.

- Add tomato/pepper mixture, maggi or knorr cubes, palm oil and mix thoroughly; (add little water if needed for loose porridge); cover and cook until yam is soft at low heat. Stir occasionally during cooking to avoid burning.

- Mash some of the pieces of the yam, add crayfish and mix thoroughly; then steam for 10 - 15 minutes at low heat.

Serve with dodo (fried Plantain) and fish or meat fried stew.

Mixed Beans and Sweet Corn Porridge

Ingredients:

1 lb. bag blackeye peas or African Red Beans

1 15¼ oz. can sweet corn or 2 cups fresh corn

1 tablespoon ground crayfish

1 15oz. can tomato sauce

1 tablespoon tomato paste

1 small onion

Garlic - to taste

Fresh ginger - to taste

2 habaneras pepper (hot, adjust to taste)

2 maggi or knorr cubes

1/3 cup palm oil or ¼ cup of oil

Water

Salt to taste

Instructions:

Step 1

- Blend tomato sauce, paste, onion, ginger, garlic and habanera peppers together. Add very little water during blending; but enough for blade to rotate. Set aside.

- Cover beans with water and bring to boil; drain and repeat this process twice. This will clean beans and reduce foaming.

- Add four (4) cups of water and cook beans until soft and tender. Add more water if needed to cook the beans.

- Reduce heat to low heat, add mixture of pepper/tomato, ground crayfish, maggi cubes and mix thoroughly; cook 15 minutes; occasionally mix to prevent burning.

- Add sweet corn, palm oil and simmer for 10-15 minutes at low heat

- Add salt to taste and water if needed; simmer for 5 minutes.

Serve with Obe Ata (Pepper Stew sauce), bread, Dodo or tortilla chips.

Ekuru and Fried Stew (Steamed Savory Beans and Pepper Stew)

Ingredients:

1 lb. bag blackeye peas or African Red Beans

1 tablespoon ground crayfish

2 pieces dry fish

1 small onion

2 habaneras pepper (hot, adjust to taste)

2 maggi or knorr cubes

1/3 cup palm oil or ¼ cup of oil

Water

Salt to taste

Instructions:

Step 1

Cleaning of the Beans

- Soak blackeye peas in cold water for about five minutes. (This will allow the beans to swell up and make it easy to remove the outer coat); or pour small amount of the beans into the blender, cover with water; grind for about 3 – 5 seconds (do not blend) and pour the beans into a large bowl; continue the process till finish.

- Cover beans with water; rub beans in between palms of both hands back and forth in the water to loosen the outer coat. The outer coat will naturally float to the top.

- Use a strainer to separate beans from the outer coat by draining the floating coats. Continue this process until beans is cleaned and no more coats or dark sport. Filter and change water as many times as needed.

Blending Clean Beans

- Blend the beans into smooth paste (add water as needed for the blender to rotate). However, do not add too much or it will become watery. **The beans batter (paste) should be a little thinner than cake batter.**

Step 2

- Make pouches/pockets with aluminum foil or use individual non-stick cup-cake cups.

- Pour blended beans into a mixing bowl and mix well till it is well aerated and light. Use warm water if needed gradually).

- Scoop beans mixture into the aluminum pouches one by one; fill it half-way to allow room for expansion during cooking. Seal the foil at the top by folding several times.

- Arrange into a deep cooking pot and add about 4 cups of water. Add more water as needed. Cook for 30 - 45 minutes; open one to check if it is done. It should be firm to the touch when cooked.

Step 3

Making the Sauce

- See Ata Din-din (Fried Pepper Sauce) Section. Use dry fish or dry shrimp in it.

- Open some of the cooked Ekuru and mash in a bowl; add ata din-din and mix thoroughly then serve.

Serving Suggestion: serve with Éko (Corn Powder Jell) or eat alone.

Water-Yam Porridge (Ikokore)

Ingredients:

1 large Water-Yam	2 habanera or chili peppers (hot, adjust to taste)
2 pieces dried fish – shredded	1 red bell peppers
1 Tablespoon ground crayfish	3 maggi or knorr cubes
1 15oz. can tomato sauce or 3 large fresh tomatoes	½ cup palm oil or 1/3 oil
3 tablespoon tomato paste	Water
1 medium onion	Salt to taste

Instructions:

- Blend tomato sauce or fresh tomatoes, tomato paste, onion, habanera peppers, and red bell peppers. Add enough water for the blade to rotate during blending; set aside.

- Peel water-yam; wash in cold water; grate into a clean bowl and season with 2 maggi or knorr cubes (crush first).

- Roll grated yam into small balls and set aside.

- Pour blended tomato/pepper mixture into a cooking pot; add crayfish, maggi or knorr cubes, dried fish, palm oil and 2 – 3 cups of water; stir and cook for 20 minutes.

- Reduce heat to low heat and drop each water-yam ball into the simmering soup to form dumplings.

- Cover the pot and steam for 30 minutes or till yam is cooked. Open and mix Porridge thoroughly to mix all the ingredients together. For loose Ikokore add very little water.

- Add salt if needed to taste; mix and stem for another 5 minutes.

Serve hot.

Nigerian Cabbage Salad

This is a mixture of raw vegetable and fruits and cold and hot.

Serves many

2 cans baked beans

1- 2 cans mackerel or sardine fish

3 - 4 eggs – Boil and Sliced

1 cabbage – shredded

3 pieces carrot - shredded

2 cucumbers - diced

3 Fresh tomatoes - diced

1 large green pepper - diced

1 large red pepper - diced

1 small red or yellow sweet onion - sliced

Mayonnaise - to taste

Instructions:

- Boil water and add to shredded cabbage in a bowl and soak for five (5) minutes; drain and dry to remove excess water from the cabbage.

- In a mixing bowl, combine cabbage, carrot, cucumber, green and red pepper, onion and toss.

- Add baked beans and mix; then add mayonnaise (to taste) and mix thoroughly.

- Add fish and mix thoroughly; garnish with sliced eggs and diced tomatoes.

- Keep in the fridge till ready to serve.

Roasted Plantain and Peanuts

Ingredients:

2 semi-ripe Plantains

Peanuts

Instructions:

- Roast plantains in the oven or on the grill and serve hot.

- Serve with peanuts, butter or margarine.

Roasted plantains go well with roasted meat.

Chin-Chin

Ingredients:

5 cups All-purpose flour

2 cups unsalted butter or margarine – cubed and keep cold

4 Egg yokes

8 Tbsp. cold water

1 cup Sugar or to taste

Instructions:

Step 1

- Combine flour and butter in a mixing bowl and knead; then add egg yolks, sugar, and knead the dough.

- Add the cold water gradually little by little into the dough and knead to form soft but firm dough.

- Roll dough into a ball and wrap with clear plastic wrap and let it rest for about three (3) hours in the fridge.

Step 2

- Then divide dough into 8 or 10 balls.

- Sprinkle some flour on a cutting board or other flat surface.

- Place one dough ball on the cutting board and flatten till it is about ½ inch thick.

- Cut into ropes then cut into little squares, each square about ½ inch by ½ inch thick or preference. Continue the process.

Step 3

- Use a deep fryer or deep cooking pot; on a medium heat place some oil on the stove and allow it to heat up.

- Once oil is hot, place a few handfuls of the cut dough into the oil (The oil may foam up, this is okay; mix with a utensil gently and the oil will come down).

- Allow the chin-chin to deep fry until light or golden brown. Stir the chin-chin while frying to prevent burning.

- Place some napkins on a flat tray, scoop fried chin-chin on it to soak up extra oil and cool down on a flat tray.

- Store in a dry airtight container.

Eat as snack.

Oblong-shaped Dodo (Fried Plantain)

Ingredients:

6 green unripe Plantains – sliced very thin

Salt to taste

Oil to fry

Instructions:

- Peel and slice the green plantains as thin as possible.

- Sprinkle with salt to taste.

- Use a deep fryer or deep cooking pot; on a medium heat, heat some oil.

- Once the oil is hot, place some sliced plantains into the oil and fry until light or golden brown.

- Remove plantains and place on paper towels to absorb the excess oil and cool.

Enjoy.

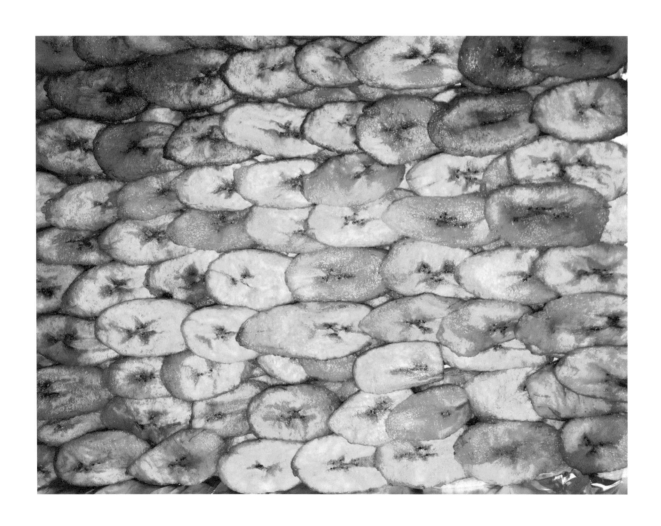

Kokoro – Corn Four Chips

Ingredients:

2 ½ cups Corn Flour	Oil
1 cup Gari	Salt
1 cups sugar or to taste	Water

Instructions:

- Boil about four (4) cups of water.

- Add some water to the corn flour and mix as you add water. You want firm dough, so don't add too much water.

- Allow to cool slightly.

- Add gari and sugar; mix thoroughly with your hand to get a firm and smooth mixture (dough).

- Cut dough into several balls.

- Sprinkle some flour on a cutting board or other flat surface; roll out each dough ball to about 3 inches long; then join both ends to form a ring.

- Use a deep fryer or deep cooking pot; on a medium heat, heat oil.

- Once the oil is hot, place some Kokoro into the oil (The oil may foam up this is okay; mix with a utensil gently and the oil will come down).

- Allow the Kokoro to deep fry; continuously stir the Kokoro gently to prevent burning.

- Remove Kokoro and place on paper towels to absorb the excess oil and cool.

Enjoy.

Nigerian Coconut Candy

Ingredients:

1 head - Fresh Coconut

Coconut Juice - from the coconut

1 cup Sugar - adjust to taste

Water

½ teaspoon salt

Instructions:

- Break the coconut - Collect the coconut juice.

- Remove the flesh from the shells and cut into tiny pieces. The best way to cut the coconut flesh: slice into thin strips first, then stack few pieces together and chop across in tiny pieces. Continue the process till finish.

- Wash and rinse the cut coconut; pour into a medium deep cooking pot; add coconut juice and about half cup of water, salt and sugar and cook at medium high on the stove.

- Once the coconut start boiling, stir regularly till all the water is just about evaporated.

- Reduce to low heat and continue cooking and stirring. The coconut will start turning brown and sticking together (this is the sugar caramelizing). If it looks drying out before caramelizing takes place, add water little by little and continue stirring.

- Coconut is done when it completely golden in color.

- Turn off the heat and scoop candy onto a flat plate and leave to cool down. Serve or wrap the coconut candy in aluminum foil individually and serve.

Spicy Fried Plantains

Ingredients:

6 ripe Plantains

3 tbsp. of ground ginger or fresh ginger

1 medium onion

2 habaneras pepper (hot adjust to taste)

3 clove garlic

2 knorr or maggi cubes

Water

Oil for frying

Instructions:

Blend ginger, onion, garlic, pepper, maggi or knorr cubes and water to form a thick paste.

Peel and slice the plantains.

Then, pour the spicy mixture on the plantain and mix well to coat the plantains.

Heating the oil in a skillet and fry the plantain until each side is brown or golden brown.

Remove and place in a paper towel to absorb the excess oil.

Serve hot with White Rice, Jollof Rice, Beans or enjoy alone.

Suya – Nigerian Shish Kabob

Ingredients:

2 lbs. lean cut beef

2 cups unsalted peanuts - Grind into powder with coffee grinder or mortar and pestle

½ tablespoon hot dry red pepper (adjust to taste)

1 teaspoon ground ginger

1 sweet onion - sliced

3-4 knorr or maggi cubes – crushed

Salt as needed

Instructions:

- Wash and dry the beef; then slice very thin; skewed into metal or stick skewers and set aside.

- Combine ground peanut, crushed knorr, pepper and ginger and mix thoroughly. Divide into two (2) separate bowl.

- Coat skewed beef with half of the peanuts mixture and marinated for 1-2 hours in the fridge.

- Cooking the suya: place the suya on a hot grill and grill slowly till meat is well done; remove from the grill.

- Sprinkle Suya with the rest of the peanuts mixture all over; top with the sliced onion and serve.

There are variations and substitutions available for preparing suya.

You may use goat meat in place of the beef.

You can cook the Suya in an oven at 350-400 degrees, but don't overcook. Otherwise, the meat will dry out.

If you are using wooden skewers, be careful not to burn the woods.

Ground fresh ginger is also okay to use.

Lagos Roast

Ingredients:

18 oz – 22 oz Bone-in Beef Ribeye (USDA Choice Angus)

Your favorite spices for Barbecuing, grilling, or smoking

Directions:

1. Sprinkle favorite grilling sauce on the meat

2. Wrap the meat completely in aluminum foil.

3. Add cut onions, sliced lemon, and basil leaves.

4. Preheat oven to 400 degrees.

5. Put the wrapped meat in a large pot or baking pan.

6. Place the pan in the oven for two hours

7. Grill the meat using the instructions in the grilling section of this book.

Deji's "Crabviar" Recipe: Crab Egg Caviar

Fresh crab is a popular delicacy in Lagos. The recipe below is an adaptation of the regular process of making fish-egg caviar. Instead of using fish egg, Deji substitutes crab egg.

Ingredients:

- 1/4 pound of crab eggs (Blue crabs and Rice-field crabs are good sources of succulent eggs)

- 1/3 cup kosher salt or pickling salt

- 4 cups cold water

Directions:

1. Mix the salt and water until the salt is all dissolved. Get a large bowl of ice water ready.

2. Open the shells of the crabs and prick out the eggs gently.

3. Soak the eggs for 20 minutes in the salt water in the fridge.

4. Get the faucet running with water just about as hot as you can take it, roughly 100-120 degrees. Lay a fine-meshed sieve in the sink.

5. Dump the eggs into a colander and transfer into the bowl of ice water for 5 minutes, then return the eggs to the salt water brine. Place the eggs in the refrigerator for another 15-20 minutes. If it stays too long, it will become very salty.

6. Gently pour out the water and let the eggs drain in a sieve for 15 minutes.

7. Pour into a clean glass jar and refrigerate for about two weeks.

8. Your crabviar is ready to enjoy with crackers, bread, rice, and so on.

Deji's Special Chicken Stove Top Recipe

This is a very simple dish, but very much cherished.

Ingredients:

1 pkg. (6 oz.) STOVE TOP Stuffing Mix for Chicken

1 stick of butter (or 3 table spoon full of margarine)

One fourth (1/4) cup of cooked white rice (long grain)

Directions

On the stove, bring 3 cups of water to boil in large pot.

Add the butter or margarine to the boiling water until it melts.

Reduce heat to low.

Add stove top and mix constantly.

Note: If there is too much water, the stove will turn too mushy, soggy, or runny.

If this happens, add more stove top dressing.

The mix should have the consistency similar to thick oat meal.

Add the cooked white rice. The rice should blend in and be unnoticeable in the mix. If there is too much rice, the mixture will be too thick. The idea is to have the rice provide something like rice milk. Not too much or too little.

Turn off heat.

Cover the pot and leave on stove for about 15 minutes before serving.

This recipe requires experimentation to discover each chef's preference. Make adjustments to suit your needs. You may embellish it with your own ingredients and substitutes.

Goat Meatballs

This dish puts a different twist on meatballs and a new experience to the goat meat, which is normally eaten in chunks or cubes in the Nigerian cooking.

Ingredients:

1 cup bread crumbs	1 tsp dried parsley
½ cup water	¼ tsps. Dried oregano, crushed
2 eggs	¼ cup dried shrimp, crushed
1 lb ground goat meat	1 tsp salt
2 table spoons olive oil	Dash of pepper
¼ cup grated Parmesan cheese	Marinara sauce

Directions:

1. Combine bread crumbs and water.
2. Stir in eggs, Parmesan, herbs, salt, and pepper.
3. Add the goat meat meatballs; mix well.
4. With wet hands, form 20 to 24 small balls.
5. Heat oil and cook meatballs until brown, turning regularly, over low to medium heat.
6. Place meatballs on paper towels to absorb excess oil.
7. Heat sauce to a boil. Lower to a simmer, add meatballs, and cook, loosely covered, for 30 to 40 minutes.
8. Serve with rice. If you want a Western version, serve with spaghetti.

Deji's Pepper Tripe Recipe

Ingredients

- 2 lbs honeycomb beef tripe (cut up into small bite-size pieces)
- 1cup of virgin olive oil
- season salt (to taste)
- fresh cracked pepper (spicy to your taste)
- One large onion (Diced).
- Two large fresh tomatoes (Sliced)

Directions

1. Clean tripe thoroughly.
2. Boil tripe in water seasoned with salt, and one bouillon cube (knorr, maggi cube, etc. to preference).
3. Heat olive oil in skillet over medium heat.
4. Pour in the mixture of diced onions and sliced tomatoes.
5. Add the boiled tripe.
6. Fry over medium heat for about 5 minutes until whitish color of the tripe is gone.
7. Turn up heat to high, med-high and finish frying for another 5 - 10 minutes, occasionally stirring.
8. The longer you fry on high, the more the juice in the skillet fries out and the olive oil and seasoning come together to make wonderfully tasty crust that sticks to the pieces of tripe.
9. Definitely serve over white steamed rice. You may also eat it straight as mouth-tossed snack pieces. The pepper tripe may also be eaten with fresh-baked bread loaves.
10. Alternately, you can execute this recipe with chicken gizzards.

Deji's Brining Process

Brining is the process of soaking meats in salt-and-water mixture to make the meat juicier, tender, and tastier, but without being too salty. Brine recipes add extra flavor to meats regardless of how the meat is to be cooked. This is often used for grilling, smoking, broiling, and frying. Brining adds moisture and flavor to make any meat better. One favorite brine recipe is provided here to give meats extra ethnic kick with the added flavor of pickling spices and favorite seasonings.

Ingredients:

- 1 gallon water
- 4 cups Kosher or coarse salt
- 1/2 cup white vinegar
- 3 tablespoons brown sugar
- 1 tablespoon pickling spice
- 1 teaspoon black pepper
- 1 teaspoon allspice
- 4 bay leaves or basil leaves
- 1 teaspoon garlic powder
- 1 teaspoon tarragon
- 8 pounds of ice cubes

Preparation:

- The night before you intend to serve the meat, wash out a cooler large enough to hold the meat.
- Stir kosher salt, brown sugar, and the other ingredients together and bring to a boil in a large pot.
- Allow to cool.

- Stir in enough ice to make enough mixture to cover the meat in the cooler.

- The goal is to keep the brine below 40 degrees during the brining process. Frozen gel packs may be used, if necessary, to maintain the brine temperature without adding excessive ice, which may dilute the brine.

- Pour the brine to cover the meat in the cooler.

- Allow the meat to soak in the cold brine for 12 to 24 hours.

- Transfer meat from the cooler for roasting, grilling, baking, etc. and discard the brine solution.

- Cook meat to per favorite recipe.

Deji's African Twist to a Serbian Sausage

This recipe is specially composed and adapted, based on Internet sources, in honor of Dr. Milan Milatovic, an avowed lover of Serbian sausages. These home-made sausages can be skewered and grilled over an open fire, broiled, or pan fried. They make excellent appetizers and sandwiches.

Ingredients:

- 1 pound ground beef chuck
- 1/2 pound ground pork
- 1/2 pound ground lamb
- 1 clove garlic, finely chopped
- 1/2 cup finely chopped onions
- 1 teaspoon salt
- Finely chopped onions, for garnish

Directions:

1. Mix together beef, pork, lamb, garlic, 1/2 cup chopped onions and salt until thoroughly combined.
2. Roll meat mixture into a long, 3/4-inch cylinder. Cut links at 4-inch intervals. Or, you can use a sausage extruder. Place on plastic wrap-lined plate, cover with more plastic wrap and refrigerate for 1 hour to firm. **Note:** Sausages can be frozen at this point. When ready to use, thaw or cook from the frozen state.
3. Broil "cevapcici" on a charcoal grill or a preheated oven broiler rack coated with cooking spray 4 to 6 inches from flame, 4 minutes per side or until no longer pink in the middle. Or they can be pan fried in a large skillet coated with cooking spray over high heat for a total of about 8 minutes, turning frequently to brown all sides.
4. Serve with chopped raw onion, Serbian potato salad and pogacha bread.
5. Adapt the above recipe to whatever your available local ingredients can offer.

Deji's Baked Guinea Fowl Recipe

This recipe requires brining. The Guinea Fowl requires marinade for at least two hours (overnight is best) to make it soft and juicy. Guinea Fowl is naturally tougher than chicken.

Ingredients:

1 quart water

2 Tbsp kosher salt

1/3 cup honey

3 cloves garlic, crushed

2 sprigs fresh sage, leaves only

¼ cup apple-cider vinegar

Juice and zest of 1 lemon

2 whole guinea fowl (each sliced into two halves, bone in, skin on)

2 slices of smoked bacon, finely chopped

3 sweet potatoes, scrubbed and thinly sliced

4 medium potatoes, scrubbed and thinly sliced

1 medium onion, peeled and thinly sliced

4 cloves garlic, peeled and thinly sliced

2 sprigs fresh sage, leaves shredded

Olive Oil

Sea salt and fresh black pepper

1⅔ cups chicken broth

⅔ cup heavy cream

1 cup grated Parmesan cheese

¼ stick of butter

Instructions:

1. Mix brine in a large bowl; add guinea fowl. Cover with plastic wrap; refrigerate 2 to 8 hours.

2. Remove guinea fowl; let come to room temperature. Drain fowl; discard brine; pat fowl dry with paper towels.

3. Preheat oven to 350 degrees.

4. In a roasting pan, toss the bacon, vegetables, garlic, and sage with olive oil and a pinch of salt and pepper. Pour in broth. Cook the vegetable mix in oven for 30 minutes.

5. Remove vegetable mix pan from oven; pour in cream and sprinkle with pepper and Parmesan.

6. Add guinea fowl, patting each piece with butter.

7. Bake in oven for 35 minutes or until guinea fowl is golden brown to your liking.

Note: Go easy on this recipe. Guinea fowl is quite expensive, costing as much as $16 per pound. The consolation is that guinea fowl is lean and tasty. It is a delicacy often reserved for special occasions. Guinea fowl is also a healthy substitute for chicken flesh in Nigerian soups.

Deji's Nuwave Roast Duck

Deji absolute enjoys roasting duck, goose, or Cornish game hens in his Nuwave oven, which uses infrared technology to cook faster and more efficiently than a conventional oven. Below is one of his favorite duck roasting recipes.

Ingredients

- 1 (6 pound) duckling
- 1 teaspoon salt
- 1/4 teaspoon pepper
- 1 onion, sliced
- 1 cup red currant jelly
- 1 tablespoon lemon juice

Directions

1. Season both the outside and inside of the duckling with salt and pepper. Place the onion inside the duck. Truss the bird and prick the skin. Dry thoroughly.

2. Nu-wave on HI for 55 minutes.

3. The duck is done to medium rare if the juices from the fattest part of the thigh or drumstick run faintly rosy when the duck is pricked. The duck is well done when the juices run pale yellow.

4. Remove the duck from the oven, discard trussing strings, and place on a serving platter. Let sit for 10 minutes before carving.

Note: If roasting goose instead of duck, cut up the large goose into four horizontal-vertical sections. Bake each section separately.

The above duck-roasting process can also be applied to rabbit or any venison.

Deji's Homemade Stockfish

Since 2000, Deji has been experimenting with and perfecting the process of making stockfish at home. Stockfish, which is a fermented air-dried Atlantic Cod, is a popular delicacy in the Nigerian diet. The fully dried fish has a strong and pungent odor, which many non-Nigerians find repulsive, but which Nigerians, particularly those from the Eastern part of Nigeria, cherish as being aromatically appetizing and gastronomically pleasing. The fresh fish is normally harvested in Norway, dried, and then exported. Once dried (with or without salt), stockfish keeps very well in the pantry. It can, thus, make a reliable food stuff during lean times. As far as he knows, Deji believes that he is the only one who has delved into the challenge of making personal homemade stockfish in North America. Something he is very proud of. It started innocently in 2000, when he mistakenly bought some whole fresh fish which, because of its frozen state, he thought was catfish. Upon thawing, he noticed that the fish had a peculiar odor and shape. The market-bought stockfish from Norway does not normally include the ugly head of the fish. So, many Nigerian who consume the commercial product have never seen a cod fish head. Deji did some research and discovered that the name of the fish he bought was Atlantic cod. In trying to find through the Internet how to cook the fish, he discovered that cod was the basic ingredient for making stockfish in the cold, cold climate of Norway. Surprised, he decided to experiment. Thus began the process of air-drying the fish by hanging it out on his backyard deck. The photo insert below shows some of the sights of commercial stockfish making operations he found on the Internet. These provided a guide for his own home experiments.

From this
(Fresh Whole Cod Fish)

To this
(Cold Air Dried Stock Fish)

Deji's homemade stock fish lab, 2017

The fish cleaning process was arduous and dirty, as the ugly fish head had to be severed in a particular pattern so that the dried carcass would have the characteristic shape of the commercial stock. Gutting the fish was also messy because many of them contained oblong-shaped egg pouches that stink bad when thawed from the frozen state.

Deji's first fish-drying experiment was a disaster because he put the fish out to dry during the hot summer months of Knoxville, Tennessee in 2001. The fish quickly rotted, instead of drying out to a stockfish form. Not only that, nocturnal animals quickly found the hanging fish as an easy source of daily meal. Deji, subsequently, improvised a wire-mesh cage and figured out that Winter-time outdoor air drying was the way to go. He has, since then, engaged in the annual ritual of buying the fresh full-headed fish from a particular Asian store in Knoxville, TN (Oriental Super Mart on Sutherland Avenue). In recent years, the availability of fresh whole cod fish has been severely limited. Inquiries revealed that the scarcity is due to overfishing the rare fish, which is quickly moving toward extinction. This has drastically increased the market price of commercial stockfish, which was not cheap to begin with. Interestingly, after experimenting with a large variety of fishes, Deji has not found any other fish that has the unique drying properties of cod. Most of them rot before they dry or dry regularly without the fermentation aroma, which is desirable just as the fermentation of corn into alcohol produces aromas of desirability to the consumers.

Cod is multi-faceted fish that is favored for a variety of uses, beyond just food products. Almost every part of the fish is used for one thing or another. Growing up in Nigeria, we remember the frequent uses of cod liver oil as a medical remedy and hailed for its health benefits. For its wide usage the fish is periodically over-fished, thus necessitating occasional fishing moratorium around the world. Fortunately, the fish is resilient and it often rebounds with plentiful opportunities for additional harvesting.

Home-grown Hot Pepper

Deji also takes delight in growing organic pepper at home every summer since 2002. This started when, during his son's (Tunji's) soccer tournament trip to Johnson City in East Tennessee in the Summer of 2002. The family had lunch at a Chinese restaurant in the city, which the red bloom on an indoor pepper plant adorned the entrance of the restaurant. Knowing what he intended to do (likewise), Deji asked for just one lobe of the pepper plant. Upon getting home, he started cultivating the pepper plant. This has become an annual ritual since then. Although he doesn't know the exact botanical name of the pepper plant, he investigated and surmised that the plant is a cultivated variety of Capsicum annuum or a variety being var. glabruisculum. Some photos of the plant are provided below. Of equal interest is Deji'2010 experiment of growing the African yam in his backyard. Needless to say, the experiment, deprived of a real tropical weather, only produced stunted tubers, not fit for human consumption. The tall pole-brazed yam plant is shown in the second picture in comparison to the pepper plant.

Tasty Spicy Meat & Fish Snacks

An amalgamation of the various recipes and instructions presented so far can be adapted for creating tasty and spicy meat and fish snacks. The key is to be creative in trying new ways of concatenating ingredients. Turkey tails, goat meat chunks, chicken gizzards, smoked fish, roasted rabbit, and rice platter are all fair game for culinary experimentations.

Printed in the United States
By Bookmasters